ESSEX AND SUFFOLK BOATYARDS AND BOAT BUILDERS

ESSEX AND SUFFOLK BOATYARDS AND BOAT BUILDERS

MIKE DAVIES

DEDICATION

THIS BOOK IS DEDICATED TO my mother and late father who, without knowing it at the time, brought us up in an environment that was to mould our lives for ever.

They gave us a freedom in our early childhood years, which helped to develop confidence and skills in all of us, which we take through life today.

Michael C Davies Wivenhoe 2008

First published in 2009 by Michael C Davies
Copyright 2009, 2019 © Michael C Davies
www.eastangliaboatbuilders.co.uk

All rights reserved

This edition published by Boatswain Books • boatswainbooks.uk
Designed and produced by Robert Deaves

ISBN: 978-1-912724-10-9

All rights reserved. No part of this publication may be reproduced, stored in a retrieval system or transmitted in any form by any means, electronic, mechanical, photocopying, recording or otherwise without the prior written permission of the publisher, the author and any other copyright holders.

CONTENTS

Preface to This Edition		7
Introduction		9
Chapter 1	Life on an Island and the early years	13
Chapter 2	Rivers Ore and Alde	30
Chapter 3	The River Deben	35
Chapter 4	Harwich Harbour, the River Stour and River Orwell	48
Chapter 5	Walton Backwaters	68
Chapter 6	The River Colne	78
Chapter 7	The River Blackwater	111
Chapter 8	The Rivers Roach and Crouch	154
Chapter 9	Leigh-on-Sea and Canvey Island	183
Chapter 10	Reflections	216
Acknowledgments		218
Index		219

PREFACE TO THIS EDITION

THIS FASCINATING RECORD OF THE boatyards and boat builders of Essex and Suffolk and its many beautfiul rivers and estuaries was first published in 2009 in A4 format. The original print run was sold in chandleries and bookshops across the region, and when they were gone, copies were later made available on DVD, but it is now available again in print, albeit in a slightly smaller format.

In the decade since the first edition, much has changed along the Essex and Suffolk coastlines. Many of the yards described herein no longer exist. However, no attempt has been made to update the content – it remains a valuable record of the history of the golden age of boat building and yachting on the East Coast.

The Publisher

YACHT BROCHURES AVAILABLE

Scanned copies of all the yacht designs in this book are available from the following website for a small fee.

Website: http://www.yachtbrochures.t83.net

INTRODUCTION

THIS BOOK IS WRITTEN FROM memories, photographs, drawings and brochures collected by the author over a period from 1944 to 2007, all in the public domain.

Some reproduced photos are of poor quality due to their age or camera (a Kodak box camera in the early years) used at the time and scanned images from old photographs and drawings.

The author wishes to thank all those who have helped in the production of this book, confirming information, dates and supplying other useful stories and anecdotes.

There have been large changes in yacht building over the years as can be seen in these pages.

The author was lucky to be born at a time when Thames Barges were still trading, smacks were still trawling for fish and boatyards were still building wooden yachts.

He saw the transition from wood to glass fibre in the late 1950s and indeed built some dinghies in glass fibre himself in the late 1960s. Ferro cement, which had been used as far back as the late 19th century, reappeared in a rush in the mid 1970s but soon petered out, leaving many part complete craft in front gardens. Steel and aluminium also saw revivals but glass fibre is today the most commonly used material.

Sailcloth is now almost entirely made in a form of Terylene, with another synthetic material, Duradon, being used particularly for larger working craft.

Stainless steel has virtually replaced galvanized iron (a material which stood up well to marine use and could be re-galvanized or painted). Plastic appears in fittings above and below the waterline.

Paints, too, have been improved considerably over the years, with a huge choice of finishes available. A more durable type of paint has been developed – two pot polyurethane and two pot epoxy.

Antifouling paints have gone through great changes, the biggest being forced upon the industry after TBT (a very effective anti fouling) was banned, as it was believed to cause severe problems to the eco systems in rivers and estuaries.

I remember discussing this at a Southampton Boat Show just after it had been banned.

A short way up from the show area was moored a huge oil tanker, reputably antifouled in TBT, as it appeared commercial vessels were still allowed to use it.

It had been calculated that this one vessel had as much anti fouling on her bottom as many of the yachts in the Solent at the time.

Most yachts today have efficient diesel engines whereas years ago the petrol and paraffin engines were more common. The modern marine diesel is quiet, economical and less pollutant. Outboards too have improved generally, getting lighter, quieter and cleaner to operate. I well remember the good old Seagull outboard and used them on various yachts and even ran some on hire boats whilst in Bedford. Their exposed flywheel where one wrapped the starting cord was always a potential source of danger. Later models were fitted with a re-coil start system that gave some protection to the flywheel.

On one occasion at Brightlingsea, on a very cold November morning, I had arranged to meet a man to take him out to view a yacht on the trots. We got into the dinghy on the hard and I pushed off with an oar to a depth sufficient to lower the Seagull and start it. All ready and on choke, I dropped the oar and pulled the starting cord. The engine fired immediately but grabbed the cord and on the first revolution of the flywheel, the cord, complete with wooden ball on the end, flew round and cracked me hard on the knuckle of my right hand. I was too occupied in navigating through the many moored dinghies to be aware of anything apart from excruciating pain. After we cleared the hard I had time to look at my hand and was amazed to find no damage whatever. I had been lucky.

In the days when I started sailing, navigational instruments were basic. A compass, lead line, chart, dividers and parallel rules. The echo sounder was, to me, one of the more useful electronic innovations of the day, giving a constant accurate measurement of depth. RDF was another gadget that came along but this was replaced by GPS, which is reputed to be accurate to within a few yards. So accurate in fact that one unfortunate yachtsman recorded a navigation buoy as a waypoint and was very surprised when his yacht ran straight into it.

All these modern electronics are without doubt very useful and most of us use them.

But I can't help thinking that years ago it all seemed far simpler, except of course when in the middle of a thick fog or making a landfall after a night at sea and not being too sure of your position.

A final item that has made life at sea more comfortable is the modern oilskin or wet weather gear as called today. Very water and wind proof and breathable too, also shoes and boots that offer excellent non-slip qualities and socks and gloves, which keep the extremities warm and dry.

The East Coast is a myriad of tidal estuaries and creeks in which many boatyards were established. Today a great number of these boatyards have disappeared, being replaced with housing.

The following chapters recall many of these boatyards and boat builders and some of the yachts they built, both those still existing and those lost to time. No attempt has been made to list all yachts built by these yards and boat builders – a record of these can be found in Lloyds Register of Yachts 1878 to 1980.

For the author it was a period of great enjoyment working around the boatyards, creeks and estuaries of the East Coast, sometimes sitting on a remote seawall or beach, eating a sandwich and listening to the gurgle of the incoming tide, the rustle of the wind in the sea lavender and the cry of the plaintive curlew across a creek.

He is honoured to have met so many skilful and characterful people over the years this book covers.

CHAPTER 1

LIFE ON AN ISLAND, EARLY DAYS OF SAILING AND STARTING WORK

I WAS BORN IN 1941 IN Wiltshire, the second of five boys to Norman and Mary Davies.

At an early age, around three years old, I first encountered water in the form of a small brook, which flowed at the bottom of our garden. My elder brother Peter, younger brother Robin and I would splash around in the brook and move stones around making dams.

In 1945, at the latter end of the war, we moved to East Mersea, near Colchester, a small hamlet of houses, one pub and a post office at the eastern end of Mersea Island, some ten miles south of Colchester in Essex.

This move was decided on as my father, who worked as a scientist for the government in London, wished to extend his sailing and also be able to commute to London.

The environment and the experiences, which followed, were to sow deep seeds inside my brothers and me and influence us on our choices of work and pleasure in the future.

The Moorings, East Mersea

Sailing would become not only a hobby for us all but a way of life and living for four of us - the fifth brother and only one to go to university, entering the teaching profession.

In these austere days, my father commuted from East Mersea to Colchester (to catch the train to London) on a Velocette motorcycle. We all rode on this, especially when a haircut was deemed necessary. He placed one of us on the petrol tank and one on the pillion and zoomed us off to Mr. Wass the barber in West Mersea. What happy days they were. I still ride motorcycles today.

The new surroundings were heaven for small boys. And we were the only children in the area at this time – a fact that would rebound on us occasionally in the future when an unexplained misdemeanour was blamed on us.

On the sea front at East Mersea, as in many other coastal areas, the government had built various coastal defence constructions to house and service naval guns. These guns were still in place when we arrived, but were removed soon after the end of the war.

The area near Cudmore Grove, then a substantial wood of oak and beeches and now completely disappeared into the sea, was dotted with army huts, some three stories high and some with steel doors. There was also a small network of tunnels linking some of them to a small underground hospital – I vividly remember a large red cross on one of these subterranean doors.

We three boys who were old enough to roam (and we did quite

freely in those days) would explore the old army installations and when we were joined a little later by our fourth brother, now old enough to keep up with us, we scoured the area collecting spent bullet cases, which being brass were readily purchased by a local scrap dealer in Colchester.

Our scavenging extended out on to the mud flats off Cudmore Grove, as we had discovered, on a very low springtide, the remains of an air gunnery target, the 'Molliette', one of two concrete ships built some years earlier and used by the Royal Air Force for target practice. This was also a good location for lobsters.

Sailing in the canoe

All across these mud flats, which comprised of deep dykes amongst sea grass covered hillocks (now all disappeared) we searched and retrieved boxes of brass cannon shells that well supplemented our meagre pocket money.

On occasion however, we brought home the occasional dangerous item, such as an unexploded incendiary bomb complete with fins or several clips of live ammunition. The bomb disposal unit was called to deal with these.

My father's interest in sailing continued and he was sailing a steel built sailing canoe in which some of us would venture with him, but as we grew older and larger and he nearly lost a good friend in a capsize, he decided a larger boat was required.

The whaler is launched at the Hythe, Colchester

Sailing around the East Coast

Moored up for the night

ONE SATURDAY AT breakfast he announced that he had purchased a larger boat. In a babble of questions from five sons (my mother told me that after having five sons she gave up hope of ever having a daughter) he told us the boat was a 25' ex naval Montague whaler, lying in Glasgow. He had bid blind on an Admiralty Disposal Sale. Seeing our puzzled expressions, he explained that the boat was being transported by rail to Colchester. It duly arrived at the Hythe Quay and was unloaded by steam crane on to the quay.

With no time to loose, the crane swung her out over the quayside and lowered her into the water. A great spurt of muddy water appeared from the bilges – the drain bung had been left ou.

The whaler is launched at the Hythe, Colchester.

A hasty jury rig was set up and my father and his friend Eric set off on the ebb downriver for East Mersea. We all piled into the waiting Austin taxi which had brought us all to Colchester and were driven back to East Mersea. We rushed down to the beach and soon saw this Viking like apparition appear sailing down the river Colne. She was beached on the small sandy beach at East Mersea and here started our inauguration into refitting a boat.

Scimitar's crew

I now understand why my father was delighted to have five sons.

The weeks that followed were taken up with a major scraping and repainting programme.

That summer and for the next year or so we sailed 'Scimitar', for that was her new name, all around the East Coast. She still had her original rig and a mighty iron centreplate that my father forbad any of us to get near when he was lowering or raising it. On occasions of no wind, four small boys were to be seen struggling with her long heavy ash oars to propel her where her captain commanded.

With us on these trips came our faithful dog, 'Bonzer' as he hated being left behind. My mother had the most basic facilities, cooking on a brass primus with a few pots and pans. The toilet was of course the simple and effective galvanised bucket.

When we moored up for the night or lay on the mud, as was the case, in a shallow creek, my father rigged an awning up over the boom to provide shelter for him, my mother and youngest brother and

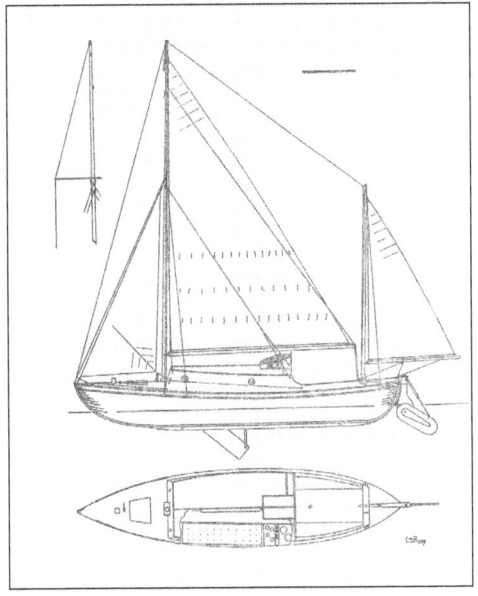

The new drawings of "Scimitar"

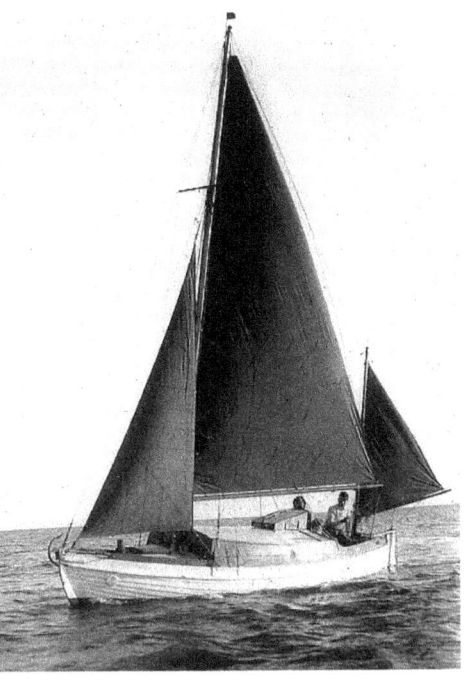

Scimitar now with cabin and new rig

Peter and Michael help lower the mainmast

Scimitar in Heybridge Lock mid 1950s

dog. The rest of us took a tent ashore and slept on the beach.

Two years later my father converted the open whaler by building a cabin on her and converting the rig to a Bermudian yawl with small ballast keel through which the centreplate passed. This improved her windward performance but still didn't allow all of us to sleep onboard. (See book written by C.N.Davies 'New Boat for Old' printed by Faber & Faber).

As we grew older and larger we helped my father more, especially with fitting out and laying up at the end of the summer. 'Scimitar' was placed in a safe mudberth for the winter, her masts removed and a winter cover stretched over her.

We had become friendly with the local farmer, Ben Spence, whose family had bought the old Golf Club, which ceased to operate after the war. He turned the greens and bunkers into farmland, partly for grain and the rest grass for grazing cattle.

One day he told us he had salvaged a large dinghy and pulled it up on the beach. Would we be interested in it?

We immediately cycled down to the beach and cast our now (we thought) experienced eyes over the craft. She was an ex barge's dinghy, heavily built with thwarts and rear seats and large iron lifting eyes fore and aft in the bilge. She had suffered some damage with most of her transom torn out and a few planks split.

The "Mersea One Design"

We went home buzzing with excitement to discuss her with our father who came down with us to look her over.

Finally we agreed to buy her for 10s 6p (about 50p today), an almighty sum for us impoverished children but it was all we could muster – three of us put up 3s 6p (about 17p) each but it bought us our first boat.

That spring and summer, in between sailing and under our father's guidance we repaired each split plank and replaced the transom.

We christened her 'Mersea One Design' and she stayed with us for many years, acting as a liberty boat at Walton-on-the-Naze, where we were now based.

In 1957, we moved to a large old farmhouse in Tendring to accommodate the growing family. A bedroom each and a range of outbuildings to accommodate our motorbikes and cars, for we had grown up somewhat.

It was at this time that a larger yacht was purchased. She was a 43' schooner, built by Dickies of Tarbet in 1907. Strongly constructed of pitch pine on oak, she had six berths and a Russell Newbury diesel engine.

She lay in a mud berth at Woodbridge on Frank Knights Quay. My mother was very pleased with the small galley area and a separate heads complete with a vintage Blake Victory toilet

We were all at boarding school by now so could only help my father at weekends during the holidays. We would discuss where we could sail in her – my father saying we could now venture abroad.

Throughout our early sailing days we had all learnt to row and scull a dinghy, tie a variety of knots, splice a rope, whip the ends of a rope and

"Lora" 43' schooner built 1907 by Dickies of Tarbet

grasp the rudiments of coastal navigation. Our main tools for the rope work are much the same today but navigation then was with a chart, compass, dividers, parallel rule and lead line.

The echo sounder had just come on to the market and this was a great aid to coastal navigation. Now we had the prospect of offshore sailing and navigating across the North Sea.

My father entered her for the first Old Gaffers Race on the Blackwater. We always attended the West Mersea Regatta, racing in the day and finishing off with visit to the fair and watching the fireworks, always a good display.

On the morning after the fireworks we would get up early and go off in the dinghy to retrieve spent rocket sticks before sailing back to Walton-on-the-Naze. 'Lora' was kept on one of Frank Halls moorings in the main channel at Walton-on-the-Naze, in the days when there were much less yachts moored there than today.

The time came for out first voyage abroad, across the North Sea to Holland.

We set off from Walton-on-the-Naze on a late Friday afternoon for a night crossing to Vlissingen. It was a fair wind with good visibility.

Sailing on "Lora"- Michael, Robin and Richard

My father had worked out a course from the Sunk lighthouse to the North Hinder. During the night, which remained clear, we could keep the loom of the Sunk astern and after a few hours we picked up the loom of the North Hinder. Today Lanbie light buoys have replaced most lightships and with less powerful lights, so to use their loom would not be possible today. In any event, most people nowadays will use a GPS, which certainly takes any guesswork out of the equation.

Landing on foreign soil was a great adventure and after clearing customs we travelled up the canal to Middleburg and on to Veere and Goes.

After a very enjoyable few days in Holland we returned to Vlissingen to prepare for our trip home across the North Sea. This was to test 'Lora' and us to our limits.

The weather had deteriorated over the previous three days and we lay in Vlissingen until the shipping forecast predicted a lull between two weather fronts. The decision was made to go and about halfway across, the weather really started to change for the worse with a stiffening southerly wind gaining strength by the hour until around midnight a full-blown gale was blowing.

With two reefs in the large mainsail, 'Lora' battled on through the night, occasionally falling off a large wave with a crash that sent a shudder through her ageing timbers.

Our watches were two hours on two hours off with two people on deck together. No one got any sleep that night.

It is interesting to note our wet weather gear of the day. A sou'wester with a suit of Yarmouth black oilskins, unlined and letting in water all over. Compared with today's sailing gear ours was very ineffectual.

bryant's boats
boat builders and hirers — bridge boathouse, bedford
props. mike davies — tel. bedford 68840 day

Bryants Boats, Bedford 1966

As the murky night gradually grew brighter with the dawn, the extent of the breaking seas became apparent. Great rolling waves with breaking crests of white foam and spray being whipped off these crests. At least at night one was unaware of this fearful vision.

'Lora' was tiller steered and I recall I had blisters on both hands.

We were all very thankful to enter Harwich harbour and wait the tide into Walton-on-the-Naze.

As time passed, we all found work in various capacities. I joined Michelin Tyre Company Ltd and spent nine months in their London office, then took up a position in the newly opened office and service premises on Gosbecks Road, Colchester.

Same location in 2005 from across the River Ouse

I then moved back to London for more training and was sent to East Yorkshire as their area representative. After nine months I moved south to Bedford and it was this move that changed my whole life.

I had dinner with old family friends who

Ranger Boats

Boat Builders & Dealers
Pilcox Hall, Tendring, Nr. Clacton−on−Sea, Essex.   Tel: Weeley 333

mentioned that the local boat builder, and hire operator, Ernie Bryant, had recently died and his widow wished to sell the business, Bryant's Boats. A bell went off in my head and the next evening I went to see Mrs Bryant and agreed to buy the business. This was in February 1965.

Ranger 14 dinghy c1967

I had very little money but undaunted, arranged to see my local bank manager (in those days you had easy access to him). He listened to my verbal business plan (I didn't know that that was what I was presenting at the time) and he agreed to lend me the money if I could find some form of security. I came out of the bank on this blustery February day with one half of me wondering what I had done and the other half elated with the new venture in front of me. My father agreed to be my security and the loan was finalised and I bought the business. To put it in perspective, I could have bought a brand new three bed-roomed detached house.

I gave in my notice to Michelin and a very understanding boss agreed to pay me up to the end of the month but let me go straight away. I had a load of work to do in a few weeks as Easter was the traditional time to open the business for the summer. I just made it and then sat and watched it rain for two solid weeks, during which my fleet of some twenty Edwardian mahogany skiffs gradually filled up with water. Then the sun came out and we had a beautiful summer.

After two years and much hard work repairing and maintaining the

Ranger 14 Prototype Sailing Dinghy

Anthony, Robin and Michael at London Boat Show 1969

boats, I built the mould for a fourteen foot glass fibre dinghy with the view to gradually replace my ageing wooden fleet – the idea was to build a mould which could be extended from 14' to 18', thus creating two models. However the first boat was so attractive that I placed an advertisement in the then Light Craft magazine and the orders flooded in.

I called these dinghies the Ranger 14 and built them under Ranger Boats.

A sailing dinghy followed, using the same hull, with ply decks and mahogany trim and alloy centreplate.

These were exhibited at the London Boat Show in 1968 and 1969 with modest success. Whilst at the Boat Show I called on Harry Sykes who built wooden dinghies in Broxbourne

Club Rescue Launch based on Colvic 19' 6" hull

and from whom I had purchased one or two hire boats earlier. I asked him how you made a million pounds in the boat business. His reply was "You start with two million and may end up with one million if you are lucky."

At 1969 Boat Show my stand was adjacent to Coast Catamaran Corporation, who were builders of and displaying the Hobie Cat 14. This unique catamaran had been designed by Hobie Alter, a Californian surfing champion, to use in the surf. As such it had no dagger boards, the lateral resistance being achieved through the asymmetric shape of each hull. The rudders also had special hinges so that on striking the beach they would fly up.

I took on the UK Agency for these catamarans with a colleague on the South Coast and we imported a dozen from Australia where they were also being built, as the import duties from USA were prohibitive. This agency ceased after about a year as the delivery from Australia could not keep up with orders. About ten years later they were again imported by another company, by which time the range had grown considerably.

After five wonderful years in Bedford, during which time I had found

Cray Fishing Boat built at Millman & Co, Geraldton, Western Australia

"Gretel II"- Freemantle, Western Australia 1972

myself and dispelled the Monday morning feeling for ever, I felt the time had come to move back to the coast. I sold the boat hiring business and temporally moved home to complete a 19' rescue launch for a south coast sailing club. This was a Colvic hull fitted with a Lister diesel, foredeck and side seating.

My future was uncertain but my spirit undaunted, when, after several discussions with a good friend, Eddie (recently out of the RAF), we decided to go as far as we could for the least amount of money. It had to be Australia as the £10 emigrant scheme was still in operation.

We arrived in Perth around midnight (in 1971) to be greeted with torrential rain – memories of my first week or two in Bedford flooded back.

After a few days in Perth, for we had opted to go to Western Australia, we purchased an old Holden estate car and drove a few hundred miles north to Geraldton, where nearby an old friend ran a farm at Mullawa. We rang him that evening and at 4am the next day he came barging into our hotel room looking the epitome of the Australian outback farmer, with old hat (no corks), shorts showing tanned legs and hands the size of dinner plates.

After a few weeks my two colleagues (another had since joined us) decided to head back to Perth as they had been unable to find jobs. I had been luckier as I was now working for a boat builder who specialised in cray fishing boats. These were some 30' LOA fitted with a 150hp diesel, small forward cabin and wheel shelter. They were designed to be capable of around 18 knots to out run the wave formations when coming back in to harbour.

Laurie Millman, the owner of the business was a great person and when he heard I knew a little about fibreglass we spent one evening and most of the next morning talking about his plans to start building in GRP. He asked me to set up the GRP side of the business. After much thought, I declined his offer as I had only been in Australia for three months and was not ready to settle down. I packed up working with Laurie at Christmas and drove back to Perth and met up with Ed and Bob and now Martin who had arrived from UK.

Marine Traders first office in Wivenhoe

We did various jobs but ended up working on the site of the new university in Perth. Our work comprised of erecting all the double skinned partition walls in the five-storey building. These were built of two skins of jarra faced plywood, attached to steel framing. I also ended up hanging all the doors. These were single and double systems made in solid jarra with safety wire glass panels – very heavy.

Whilst in Fremantle one day I came across 'Gretel I', on the slip being refitted and 'Gretel II' alongside a quay. They were two of a previous America Cup team challenge.

This contract ended and about this time I received a letter from my brother Peter, who had been skippering Captain Burkes Windjammer fleet out of Miami and around the West Indies. He had this idea of buying a cargo ship as he felt the local West Indian wooden schooners were slow and unreliable.

The Old Chapel – home and office from 1979-1982

Marine Traders offices 1982 –1987

The idea appealed and I bought my ticket home (and had to repay the government for the flight out) sailing from Fremantle on a Greek ship to Singapore, meeting up with an old friend there and then onwards to London by plane.

We did buy a coaster in Denmark and I spent a couple of months working it with Peter but decided it was not the life for me. So I quit after we arrived at Colchester for Christmas 1972.

I was back on the beach but I had an idea I had been brooding on for a few weeks.

This idea hatched in to my next business, which I was to run for many happy years as a yacht broker. In 1973, I set up Marine Traders Yacht Brokers, working solely on the East Coast, from Kings Lynn to Southend-on-Sea.

My main remit was to be able to sleep in my own bed at night.

With a tight budget I was lucky enough to have a brother in Wivenhoe who rented me a small room in his property in West Street. I worked here from 1973 to 1977.

In 1976 I got married and needed to provide a home. I had met Naval Architect and Designer, David Cannell, who had purchased an old chapel earlier – we agreed to develop it together and over the course of two years transformed the derelict building into two homes, with offices for each of us. The building was split down the middle and a dividing wall built up the centre. The Congregational

Same building in 2008 refitted at luxury apartments

Chapel was built in 1846 and had survived the great earthquake in the late 1800s. I lived and worked here until 1982.

I moved house and my office was relocated to Wivenhoe quay, in

Marine Traders brokerage and chandlery at Titchmarsh Marina 1987-2000

buildings owned by Wilkin & Sons, jam makers from Tiptree. I remember one lunch time I came down the stairs to walk home and was confronted with sea water up to the second step. My lunch was late that day. Looking out across the river, it was a beautiful place from which to work. In 2006, work commenced to convert these buildings into residential units.

In 1987 I moved my office to Titchmarsh Marina at Walton-on-the-Naze where I worked until retirement in 2000.

The many yachts, boat yards and boatbuilders I came across in the area form the basis of the following chapters – 'Essex and Suffolk Boatyards & Boat Builders'.

CHAPTER 2

SOUTHWOLD AND ALDEBURGH

SOUTHWOLD HARBOUR IS LOCATED ON the River Blyth, a tidal river in the north of Suffolk, with the river running straight in from the North Sea. The Harbour is on the North bank of the River Blyth with Walberswick on the opposite bank.

The town of Southwold lays about a mile north, between salt marshes on the left and the sand dunes and sea on the right. The Alfred Corry Museum is located by the large car park by the rivers edge before turning up towards the town.

Along the river, going inland are to be found fisherman's sheds, the ferry across to Walberswick, the Harbour Inn and Harbour Marine Services boatyard.

In the 1970s I visited the yard, then known as A.U.I. in buildings now used by Harbour Marine Services.

This yard was established in 1988 and provides full boatyard services with lifting and launching up to 30 tons. There is a large area of hard

Facilities at Harbour Marine Chandlers Offers Harbour Marine (Brokerage Ltd)

Harbour Marine Services
Southwold Harbour
Boatbuilding & Marine Engineering
Chandlery and Nautical Gifts

standing for laying up and the yard encourages their customers to make full use of the facilities and work on their own craft.

Specialising in classic yachts dating back to the early 1900s, they also work on all types of yachts and working craft built in glass fibre, steel, and ferro-cement.

Harbour Marine Services

ALDEBURGH AND THE RIVER ALDE

Coming south the next river is the Ore/Alde. The entrance is hard to locate but the Martello tower about a mile SW of the entrance shows well and north of it are some cottages. Outlying shingle banks are located at the entrance, which show clearly at low water.

Orford Quay

Slaughden Quay

The Ore and Alde are two names for the same river, the Ore being the lower part from the entrance up to Randalls Point (opposite Slaughden Quay) and the Alde carrying on up to Snape Bridge, its navigable limit.

At Orford, there are no yard facilities but the quay provides access to the river.

```
         R. F. UPSON & Co.      № 4676
      Slaughden Quay, Aldeburgh, Suffolk
         R. F. Upson    B. Upson    B. Upson
```

R F Upson & Co

R F Upson & Co

Further upstream Slaughden Quay juts out from the eastern bank of the Alde. Here R F Upson & Co's boatyard is located.

The yard was set up by Russell Upson (time served apprentice at Whisstocks, Woodbridge) and is now run by his son Brian Upson. Full facilities including winter laying up, moorings and maintenance are offered. They have also built a variety of working craft in wood and glass fibre.

Further up towards the town by the green is Aldeburgh Boatyard. Peter Wilson took over the yard in 1979, offering laying up facilities, chandlery and boat building. They have specialised in building Dragon Class, Loch Longs and 2.4 Metres as well as repair and restoration of old boats.

The navigable part of the river Alde ends at Snape Bridge where a large maltings complex is located. This has been gradually converted over to a music school

Brian Upson

Aldeburgh Boatyard

and concert hall, pioneered by Benjamin Brittan, where all types of music are catered for throughout the year, culminating in the summer concert comprising of classical music, opera, jazz and much more.

The Granary Tea Shop offers food all day and the Plough & Sail pub is next door, also offering good ales and food.

Snape Quay

CHAPTER 3

THE RIVER DEBEN

SOME FOUR MILES SOUTH OF the Ore/Alde the entrance to the River Deben is navigated through a channel carved between shifting sand bars. The river is approximately nine miles long running inland in a north-westerly direction.

At the entrance, Felixstowe Ferry is so named as there is a ferry running across from Felixstowe to Bawdsey. Bawdsey Manor was used during the war years to develop

'Lora' 43' Schooner on slip at Felixstowe Ferry c1956

'Scimitar' Crusader ashore at Felixstowe Ferry Boatyard 1985

Felixstowe Ferry Boatyard

radar for the air force and navy. The manor house is still standing as is a tall aerial.

C H Fox & Sons operated the slip at the ferry (their main yard was in Ipswich) and in 1956, shortly after my father purchased Lora, 43' schooner, I photographed her on their slip undergoing work including new keel bolts.

Felixstowe Ferry Boatyard Ltd

Trevor Moore took over the yard, later trading under this name. He built various yachts and working craft, offered laying up facilities, moorings and operated the slip.

It was here in 1985 that I purchased a Crusader Class yacht 'Scimitar' which had been ashore for a year or two and I had actually sold to a client. He sadly died on the way to take over the yacht and some weeks later I purchased her, fitted her out and sailed her to Walton-on-the Naze to my mooring.

Ramsholt

About two miles up river, on the northern bank, lies Ramsholt, a very attractive and popular location for yachtsmen. There are no yard facilities here but the harbour master George Collins runs many moorings

---

FELIXSTOWE FERRY BOAT YARD LTD.
FELIXSTOWE FERRY
SUFFOLK

Left: Ramsholt Arms • Right: Ramsholt Quay

and will locate a vacant mooring for visiting yachtsmen.

The Ramsholt Arms offers excellent food.

A couple of miles further upstream Waldringfield lies on the west bank, with the main channel of the river running close to the beach. There is another channel passing east of the island off Stonner Point but this dries at low water.

Waldringfield Boatyard

Another very attractive location, Waldringfield has one boatyard, Waldringfield Boatyard, run for many years by Ernie Nunn who built many fine wooden yachts, including Dragons.

I first met Ernie Nunn on a visit to his yard in the early 1970s. On enquiring as to where I could

Waldringfield Boatyard

WALDRINGFIELD BOATYARD LIMITED
Yacht and Boatbuilders

YACHT CHANDLERS AND BROKERS MARINE INSURANCE MOORINGS · STORAGE MARINE ENGINEERS	THE QUAY, WALDRINGFIELD Nr. WOODBRIDGE SUFFOLK IP12 4QZ
	Telephone: WALDRINGFIELD (047336) 260

VAT Reg. No. 299 9561 73

find Mr Nunn, I was directed to his house up the road. I found him gently hoeing some vegetables in his garden, for this was one of his great passions.

The yard was taken over by Mr Reg Brown and then his son Andrew. Full yard facilities are provided with moorings, winter laying up and yacht maintenance.

IN THE LATE 1970s I bought a Folkboat from this yard. Her name was 'Rodingen' and she was reputedly built in 1942 at Söderköping, Sweden.

'Rodingen' Folkboat

I started to refit her at the yard, scraping all the interior paint from her bilges and applying several coats of metallic grey primer after brushing on a coat of clear Cuprinol. I then had her transported to Wivenhoe by my brother, Peter Davies who was running Whippatts Transport at the time and unloaded at Colne Marine on the quayside at Wivenhoe where I lived. Her refit was duly finished and Guy Harding craned her in using his hand-operated crane (see Chapter 6, The Colne). I then sailed her to Walton-on-the-Naze where I had arranged moorings in the Twizzle with Frank Halls & Sons. 'Rodingen' was a very original Folkboat, built in clinker Baltic red pine on oak frames and

Martlesham Creek Boatyard

MIKE DAVIES

MARTLESHAM CREEK BOATYARD
SLIPPING, LAUNCHING, MOORINGS, CHANDLERY, FUEL, ENGINE REPAIRS AND MAINTENANCE

Reply to:
M J Ingham
Martlesham Creek Boatyard
Church Lane
Martlesham

Telephone/Fax 01394 384727
Mobile 07850 754726
e-mail - Suffolk

not fitted with an engine, electrics or marine toilet. She was the epitome of the small cruising yacht, simple but efficient. She gave us several years of happy sailing around the East Coast.

Close to the yard one can drink and dine at the Maybush Inn, with excellent views overlooking the Deben.

MARTLESHAM CREEK BOATYARD

Carrying on up river, Martlesham Creek veers off to the west. There is a small boatyard located here. Set up by Roy Ingham in 1964, offering moorings and laying up facilities. In the early 1970s his son Mike joined the business and continues to run it today, having increased the stagings and moorings. He is also carrying out conversions on steel barges. A tranquil setting that reminds one of sailing years ago.

Another mile upstream Woodbridge appears on the west bank.

EVERSON & SONS LTD

Everson & Sons Ltd appears first, originally established in 1889 by A M Everson, later run by Mr P A Darby (who ran a delightful steam yacht), then part of Frank Knights operation for some years and now independent again.

A variety of yachts were built here over many years some to the design of A. Everson, the original owner of the yard and other designers such as Maurice Griffiths.

The Deben Cherub, designed by A.R.G.Curjel was built by Everson in the 1930s This yacht is Jubilee.

Everson & Sons Ltd

Deben Cherub

Ideally suited for the rivers, creeks and the East Coast with a shoal draft and gaff rig.

This yacht is 'Nyala', again built by Everson in 1933 to a design by Maurice Griffiths.

A gaff ketch with pleasing lines and good accommodation. She has been cruised extensively.

Frank Knights

A little further upstream Frank Knights operates from the Ferry Quay. Boat builders and marine engineers, they have constructed various working craft and repaired a variety of yachts. Full yard facilities are on hand. I first met Frank Knights as a teenage boy in the late 1950s

'Nyala'

INVOICE		
LIFTING OUT (6 TONS) TOWAGE, ETC.		ENGINE SALES & INSTALLATIONS REPAIRS, INSURANCE

FRANK KNIGHTS (SHIPWRIGHTS) LTD.

FERRY QUAY, WOODBRIDGE IP12 1BW
TEL: WOODBRIDGE (0394) 382318

Frank Knights

when my father purchased 'Lora', a 43' schooner lying in the mudberth on the quay. In the course of running Marine Traders Yacht Brokers over the years we had many a chat.

This is 'Quiz', originally built in 1872 at Paglesham and rebuilt by Frank Knights.

Frank Knights died in September 2008 after running his business for many years.

The 'Quiz'

Ferry Quay

Whisstocks Ltd

Just around the corner was located Whisstocks Ltd, established in 1926 but it sadly ceased trading some years ago.

In their time they built over 500 yachts from wooden craft such as the Deben 4 Tonner designed by W M Blake and commenced in 1936 with over 40 being built over the years, both in gaff and Bermudian rigs. The Deben 6 tonner followed.

Other W M Blake designs were built, Marlin a 36.7' auxiliary cutter, 'Mirelle' a 32.4' auxiliary cutter in 1937 to name but a few. In 1952 they built 'Corista', designed by the local naval architect, J. Francis Jones, a 46.1' auxiliary cutter (see photo).

In 1979 they built their last steamed framed yacht and more modern materials were utilized, such as aluminium. This sadly was the last phase of boatbuilding at Whisstocks.

Whisstocks

WHISSTOCKS LTD
Ferry Quay, Woodbridge, Suffolk, England. Tel: Woodbridge (03943) 4222
Fax: 03943 6476   Reg in England No: 189 9426

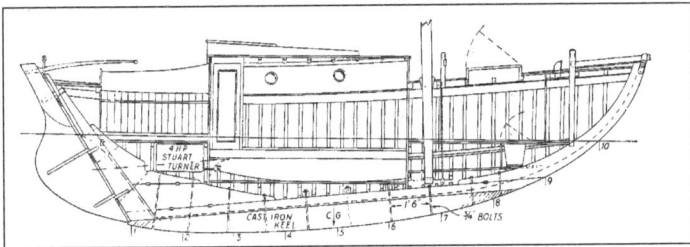

Deben 4 Tonner

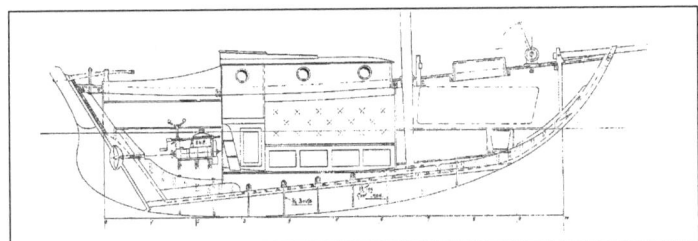

'Corista'

ESSEX AND SUFFOLK BOATYARDS AND BOAT BUILDERS

Whisstocks built alloy schooner

Adjacent to Whisstocks yard is located the old tide mill.

This was restored to full working order complete with mill pond. Next to this is the Tide Mill Marina, with a sill to retain the water level at low tide and pontoons for yachts.

This is a delightful spot to moor up overnight, afloat, to visit Woodbridge.

Continuing upstream, on the east bank is Sutton Hoo, with rolling hillocks and sandy cliffs, where in 1939 one of the most important archaeological finds was discovered. A Saxon Burial mound was excavated to reveal

Tide Mill

Tide Mill Marina

the remains of the Saxon Ship and treasure, now housed in the British Museum. A museum building has also been constructed on site with copies of the artefacts and many photographs.

ROBERSTONS BOATYARD

Opposite on the west bank is Roberstons Boatyard. This yard commenced building yachts in Ipswich in 1884, known as E J Robertson & Co and moved to Woodbridge, trading as A V Robertson. There are records of Woodbridge showing that Men of War were built on the site from 1624 to 1700 and then merchant schooners and brigs up to 1853.

They built a large number of yachts from small ones and those of 60 tons or so. Atalanta was built by them in Ipswich in 1877, being 77.4' long. The trading name changed again to Robertsons of Woodbridge

Robertsons Boatyard

(Boatbuilders) Ltd when in 1985 Mike Illingworth and Adrian Overbury took over the yard and built it up again, repairing, refitting and building new yachts. They offer mud berths on pontoons and winter laying up.

R LARKMAN LTD

A short walk along the sea wall north brings us to a yard set up and run by Dick Larkman and his son. They have a large area for laying up and a workshop in which yachts are built and repaired.

Larkman's yard

MELTON BOATYARD AND GRANARY YACHT HARBOUR

Next door is the yard which Mel Skeet & Richard Upshall took over in 1982, known as Melton Boatyard, which was then virtually derelict, changing its name later to Granary Yacht Harbour after the former granary building which is still there. Mel's son, Simon has joined the team and the facilities have been constantly improved.

MELTON BOATYARD LIMITED

Later the name was changed to:

Mel Skeet Granary Yacht Harbour

From humble beginnings the yard developed over the years

Now capable of lifting 30 tons.

CHAPTER 4

HARWICH HARBOUR, THE RIVERS STOUR AND ORWELL & IPSWICH

Harwich Harbour

THE JUNCTION OF THE RIVER Stour and River Orwell form that largest area of deep protected water on the East Coast, known as Harwich Harbour.

The entrance is through a channel (now well dredged) between Languard Point on the east side and Beacon Cliff on the west side.

Felixstowe Container Port on the east side is the largest such port in the UK handling ships which can carry 11,000 containers

The earliest mention of a harbour at Harwich is recorded in the Anglo-Saxon Chronicle dated 885.

Ships were built here in the 16th Century under Chapman and Pett. In 1561 Queen Elizabeth I came to inspect the shipyard and stayed at the house in what is known as King's Head Street.

The Shipyard was developed in 1660 and many naval ships were built

Felixstowe Docks

to the design of Anthony Deane. Samuel Pepys, the diarist was Secretary for the Navy and MP for Harwich and mentions the shipyard – he and Deane were friends and MPs.

In the 18th and 19th centuries the shipyard came under the control of the families Bailey, Graham and Bagshaw and by 1850 the family Vaux.

An interesting machine still to be seen is the The Treadwheel Crane, re-housed on Harwich Green in 1932, which spent it's working life in this shipyard from 1667 to 1927. It is believed to have been powered by men walking in the interior of the two wheels.

NELSON ALSO USED Harwich harbour for repairs and to victual his ships. The Medusa channel to the south and off the Naze at Walton-on-the-Naze was charted by him in an effort to leave Harwich harbour where he was trapped by adverse winds. The name Medusa coming from his ship at the time.

Treadwheel Crane

Naval House

Trinity House, founded in 1514 by Henry VIII has had a base here since 1812, to service the buoys in their area. The head office moved to Harwich, from Trinity Square, London, next to Tower Hill, in 1940.

Upstream from Trinity House pier is a large area of mudflats Bathside Bay, for which permission has been granted to develop it into a large container port. Upstream of this is the existing Parkeston Quay container and passenger ferries port.

In 1958 I joined David Budworth Ltd (they previously ran St Osyth Boatyard for a while) who were gas turbine engineers, located in what was the old Naval Yard on the extreme eastern point of Harwich, now a ferry terminal. When I worked here the slip was still in evidence but little used. One lunchtime I was walking near the slip at high tide and noticed a large black bulk of timber just floating. As I prodded it, a shout from David Budworth across the yard gained my attention. He came over to me and asked me if I knew what I was prodding.

I replied no, to which he replied, "That's worth more than your annual salary – pull it ashore." He then explained that it was a bulk of Lignum Vitae – I looked it up in the dictionary and thus added to the

Tug 'Kelpie'

ever increasing learning curve of a young man.

Navyard Wharf was established in 1962 and a plaque near the entrance shows a list of Men of War constructed in the Old Naval Yard 1660-1827.

IN 1962, I joined my brother Peter and colleague Mick O'Sullivan in a venture based on the tug 'Kelpie' we had hired from Knights in Rochester. The idea was to bring her to Harwich and offer a towing service with the vessel. Unfortunately we were several years too early as the development around Harwich and Felixstowe started some years later. In the late 1890s many Thames barges were built in Harwich, by J & H Cann ('Ethel' 1894, 'Felix' 1893), McClearon ('Ena' 1906, 'Dannebrog' 1901) to name but a few.

Opposite Harwich is Shotley, the home for many years of the naval training establishment, Ganges, which closed in the mid 1970s. Many of the original buildings are still there and the tall rigged white mast is still standing.

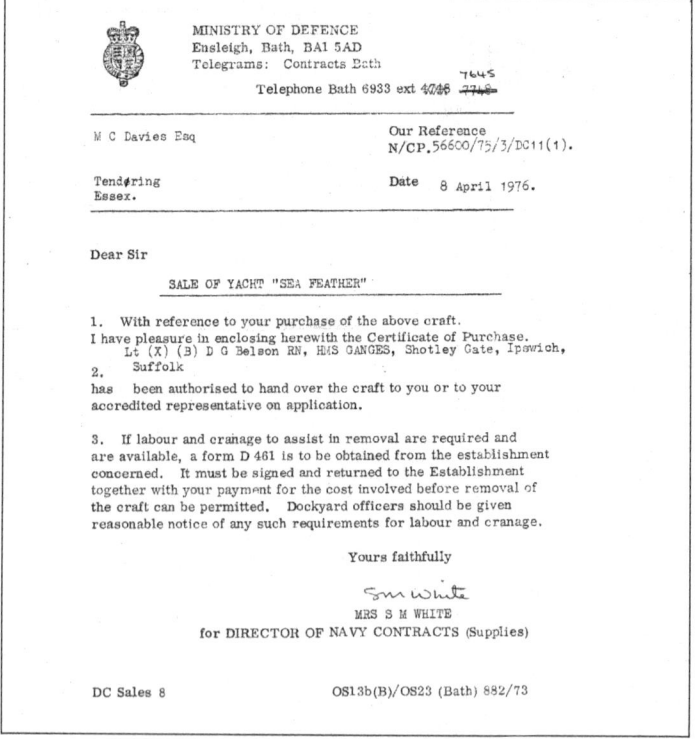

50 Square Metre 'Sea Feather'

In 1976, with a colleague, we purchased the Ganges training yacht, 'Sea Feather', a 50 square meter built by Kiel Wellingdorf in 1938, under an Admiralty Disposal Sale. She was one of many such yachts brought over here at the end of the war and known as 'Windfalls'. At this time, the then Prime Minister, Harold Wilson had levied a VAT tax of 25% on boats.

In the late 1980s Shotley Point Marina was dug out in the area of the old running track. With a large lock and dredged channel it is opera-

Lock at 'Shotley Point Marina'

The Shipwreck Bar

tional for 24 hours a day.

There are some 350 berths and a large travel lift, repair workshop and chandlery. The Shipwreck bar and restaurant serves excellent food.

The River Stour

Horlocks

Further upsteam on the River Stour and just below Mistley is located the yard originally run by Peter Horlock. The book 'Mistley Man's Log' by C H Horlock (Chub Horlock) details the barging days of the era.

Horlocks – now Mistly Marine

Richard Horlock was in Hammersmith in 1650 and the barge Experiment, 63 tons, measuring 58' x 18' with leeboards was built at Rettenden in 1791, possibly by Samuel Horlock. This is the first record of a barge being built on the East Coast.

Mistly Quay was built in 1730 by Richard Rigby. In 1770 Rigby operated a shipyard and built ships until the middle of the 19th century

John Horlock was at Mistley in 1839. In 1865 Robertson's of Ipswich built the barge Pride of Stow for Richard Horlock. In 1878 Cann's of Harwich built Horlocks the barge Volunteer, 58 tons. Canns also built shrimping bawleys and beach boats for Southend-on-Sea.

In 1919 F W Horlock started a shipyard at Mistly. David Foster took over what was remaining of the yard in 1992 and has expanded the area, built a house and continues to develop the yard with a pontoon and mudberth moorings.

At Mistly there is still a working quay where small coasters discharge their cargoes.

Above the tidal Stour, a new sluice gate system was built some years ago by Cattawade Bridge and a new road bridge, known as the White Bridge was built.

Some river barges were built and traded the Stour and in 1705 the Stour was made navigable by Act of Parliament, with 15 locks from Sudbury to Brantham. The last barge to navigate the 15 locks was in 1916 but lower stretches were worked until 1930 when last barges past

Old Cattawade Bridge

Site of Freddie Smeeth's boat building and hiring yard

through Dedham lock.

By the old Cattawade bridge there is a boat ramp for transiting from the river into the tidal part of the River Stour

For many years the Stour Restoration Society has gradually been rebuilding locks from Sudbury downwards.

In the late 1980s I paddled my Canadian canoe with my daughter through the newly opened Dedham Lock with a hundred or so other small boats to commemorate the re-opening of the lock.

'Alan III', 29' 6" x 23' 4" x 9' X 4' Draft. Carvel iroko on steamed American elm frames

G F Smeeth

Just below the lock and road bridge at Dedham was a boatyard run by G F Smeeth (Freddie) who also operated a fleet of hire rowing boats.

He built a number of wooden yachts here, 'Eliane' 31.7' by John Leather in 1959, 'Miranda' by John Leather 33.3' in 1960, 'Tasman' an East Coast One Design, 31.3 by Alan Buchanan in 1964, 'Alan III', 29.5' designed by Tom Riggs in 1972 (see photo) and a Maurice Griffiths design Kylix, 1971.

This is a 'Kylix II', 27 x 23'5" x 8' 2" x 3' built by Bure Marine, Gt Yarmouth in 1980

The hire boats are still there, although replaced by new ones some years ago, built in ply/epoxy by Colin Scattergood from Wivenhoe and there is now a first class restaurant where the old boathouse used to be.

The River Orwell

Running some nine miles in a north-westerly direction from Harwich Harbour, the River Orwell passes through much unspoilt countryside up to Ipswich.

It is a busy river with much commercial traffic and the channel is well dredged and lit.

Suffolk Yacht Harbour

On the east bank about one and a half miles upstream lies Suffolk Yacht Harbour at Levington, a tidal

Suffolk Yacht Harbour

marina offering all boatyard facilities. It was in 1961 that Michael Spear's vision of a marina began and in 1967 Suffolk Yacht Harbour Ltd was formed with Michael Spear, Charles Stennet and local boat builder Eric Wright in partnership.

After three years of hard work the first 40 berths were ready and all instantly booked.

By 1973 170 berths had been created. Jonathon Dyke has for some years been a director with Michael Spear and the marina continues to develop with good all round facilities. Specialist refit work is carried out on wooden yachts.

Just over a mile onwards Pin Mill lies on the west bank. A long established mooring area for yachtsmen there are now only two main boatyards, Harry King & Son, and Fred Webb Ltd.

Harry King & Son, set up in 1850, built many fine wooden yachts, some to their own design ('Wenonah', 6 TM, 1923), some to designs by Maurice Griffiths and the well known 'Peter Duck' for Arthur Ransome in 1946 to a design by Laurent Giles & Partners. A number of Peter

Harry King & Sons

Ducks were subsequently built by Porter & Haylett in Wroxham.

The yard is now run by Gus Curtis who carries out yacht refitting and repairs and winter laying up. With his wife Sarah they are directors of the mooring company with Tony and Christine Ward and run the moorings at Pin Mill.

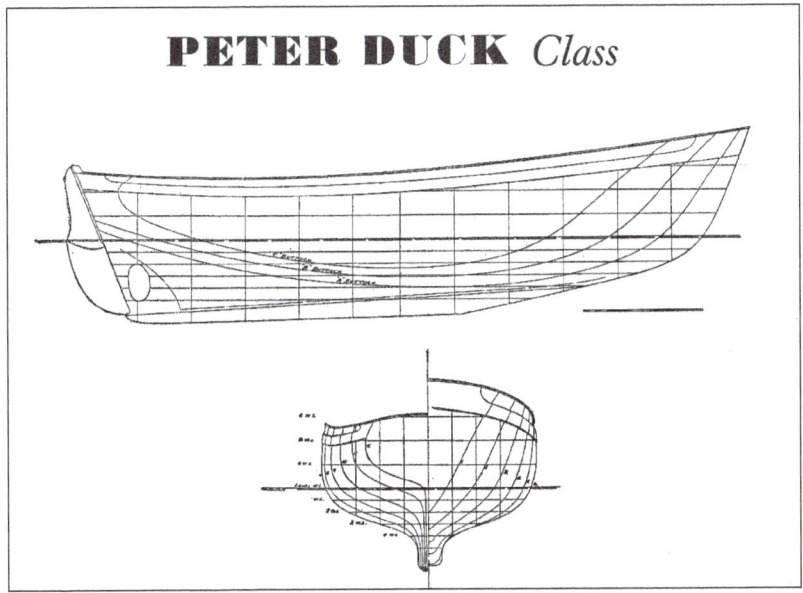

Fred Webb Ltd

Fred Webb Ltd

Fred Webb Ltd is next door downstream and in its day rebuilt Thames Barges and refitted yachts. They offer general refit work and winter laying up.

Just across the road behind the pub used to be Jack Ward & Sons, run for many years until sold by Tony Ward who had moorings and ran a rigging and chandlery from the site. The premises are now a studio and tea rooms.

On the riverside, at the top of the hard, is the well known public house, the Butt & Oyster where excellent ales and food are available.

Upstream about half a mile on the west bank lies Wolverstone Marina.

Now part of Marina Developments, the marina is set in 22 acres of delightful parkland with interesting walks and good pubs nearby. Full yard facilities are available.

Formerly Jack Ward & Sons

Butt & Oyster, Pin Mill

Woolverstone Marina 2008

Fox's Marina Ipswich Ltd
The Strand, Wherstead, Ipswich, Suffolk IP2 8SA

Just below Ipswich on the east bank lies Fox's Marina.

The name derives from C H Fox & Son Ltd who were boat builders nearby for many years – see later. The Oyster Group took over in the late 1970s and relocated here.

Full marina facilities are on hand with a large chandlery and epoxy treatment and spray painting workshops, stainless steel fabrication, electronics and rigging and brokerage.

C H Fox & Son Ltd

From premises in Wherstead Road, C H Fox & Son Ltd had been building boats for many years.

They were building from 1927 and were well known for motor cruisers built to their own designs as well as yachts. In 1931 they built 'Karen' a 22' x 6.9' motorboat to their own design. In 1933 'Sulaire' a 26.1' x 8' ketch was built. Also in 1933 to a design by T Harrison Butler, they built 'Elgris', 21' x 7' and throughout the 1930s, 1940s (boats for the Admiralty were built here during the war years), 1950s and 1960s many power

Fox's Marina

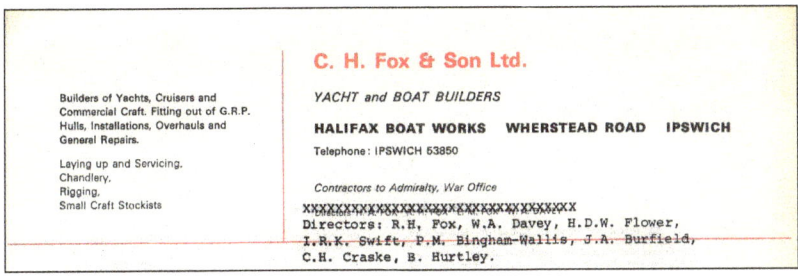

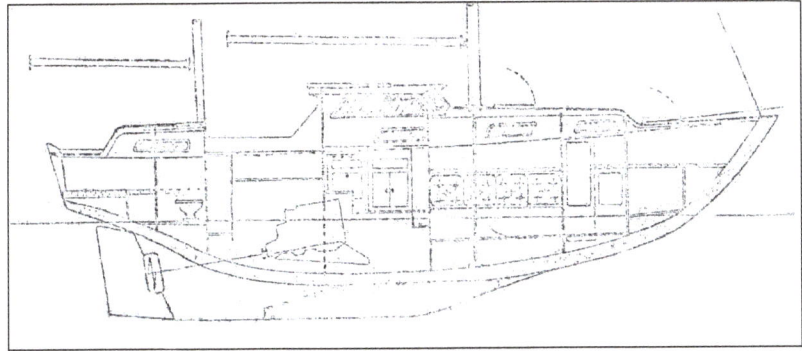

Above: Fox 35 Ketch • Below: Fox 24 Quarter Tonner

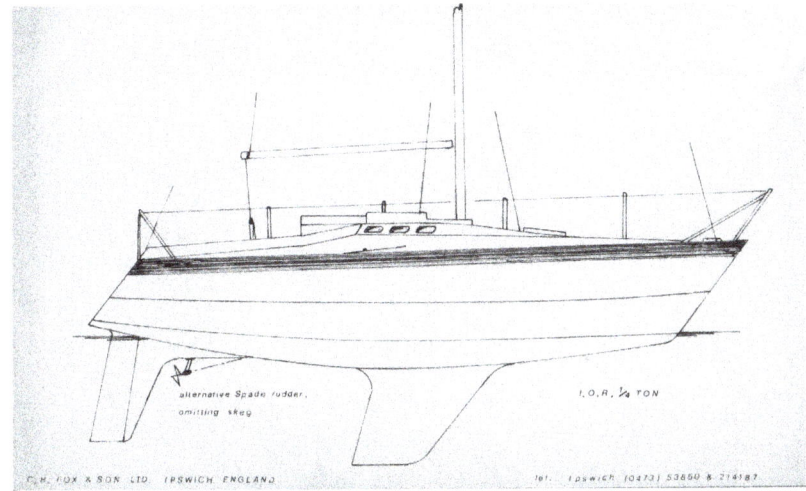

and sailing craft were built to various designers such as Robert Clarke, 1947 'Vera Jane' 24.9' x 7.9, 1953 Uffa Fox & R G Ross design 'Flying Fifty' a 61.8' x 15.5' ketch. As with most boat builders they also built in glass fibre, fitting out a hull by Halmatic in 1962 'Ilala', 32' x 9.5' an auxiliary sloop. Sometime in the late 1950s C H Fox & Son Ltd were also running Felixstowe Ferry Boatyard and slip. (See chapter 1 'Lora' on slip at Felixstowe Ferry).

In 1974 they built a Guy Thompson Quarter Tonner – see drawing on Page 63 – in plywood.

In 1975 the Fox 35 Ketch was built in strip planking, with a view to taking a mould later to build in glass fibre. The only drawing I have is of poor quality but is reproduced on Page 63..

Boat building continued through the 1970s with a Ron Holland design 'Orange Pippin' being built in 1976 – she was 30' x 10.3'. In the late 1970s the business was taken over by The Oyster Group and relocated to the current Fox's Marina (see Fox's Marina before).

Debbages Yacht Services

The old river forks off left at the lock gates and Debbages Yacht Services are on the left bank. The business was started by Denis Debbage some years ago after he ran Wolverstone Shipyard. As well as carrying out yacht repairs in a large floating steel barge fitted out as a workshop, the yard also operates a boat transport business. Denis Debbage originally set up the yard and transport business and sold to the current owners Peter and Chris Nixon in 1985.

Debbages Yacht Services- earlier photograph

MIKE DAVIES

D. DEBBAGE
YACHTING SERVICES

The Quay, New Cut West
Ipswich, Suffolk

Telephone: Ipswich 50169

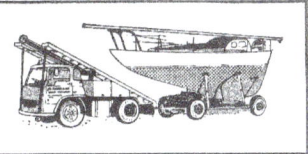

YACHT—Transport, Cranage, Repairs, Moorings, Brokerage, New Yachts   V.A.T. Reg. No. 102 0113 64

Debbages Yacht Services taken in 2007

Ipswich

The Ipswich Wet Dock itself was constructed in 1850 and was at the time the largest in Europe. It is now almost exclusively used for yacht berthing.

Ipswich Dock

Above: Ipswich Dock lock • Below: Neptune Marina

There are two marinas inside the dock.

Neptune Marina

Neptune Marina was established some years ago and has pontoon berths. Now surrounded by modern housing developments

Ipswich Haven Marina

Ipswich Haven Marina opened in April 2000 and has full facilities and pontoon moorings. It is owned by Associated British Ports.

Ipswich Haven Marina

IPSWICH HAVEN MARINA

Associated British Ports
Old Custom House
Key Street
Ipswich
Suffolk IP4 1BY

Telephone: +44 (0) 1473 236644
Facsimile: +44 (0) 1473 236645
e-mail: ipswich@abports.co.uk
www.abports.co.uk

CHAPTER 5

WALTON BACKWATERS

THE WALTON BACKWATERS IS AN area of exceptional natural beauty with many creeks and small islands, the home of seals and sea birds in abundance.

The well-known writer of children's books, Arthur Ransome, based his 'Secret Water' tale in this delightful area and his chart in the book differs little from the modern chart of today.

The entrance to the Backwaters lies some half a mile southwest from Harwich Harbour and is marked by the Pye End buoy, once hard to find but now lit and more visible. The Medusa channel to the south is the route in from the Wallet, passing the Stone Banks buoy on the way.

Entering the main channel, well marked with red and green buoys, at Island Point buoy the main channel to Walton Town forks to port whilst continuing on westerly one enters the broad expanse of Hamford Water. A short way up on the starboard side is a buoy marking the entrance to Oakley Creek, at the top of which is a quay serving the explosives fac-

The Twizzle Creek

tory on Bramble Island. A colony of seals lives in this area of creeks and saltings.

Continuing up Hamford Water, Horsey Island is located on the south side and is a farm once specialising in breeding Arab horses. The island is reached by a wade at low tide.

Landermere creek leads to Landermere Quay and above this Beaumont Creek terminates at Beaumont Quay where a plaque tells you it was constructed with stones from the old London Bridge.

All these quays were once in regular use by Thames Barges picking up various cargoes from the farms in the area.

The Walton Channel running up past Stone Point to port, now a bird sanctuary but still accessible at all states of the tide, continues south where a fork to starboard signals the start of the Twizzle Creek, which continues past the entrance to Titchmarsh Marina, one of the largest marinas on the East Coast and started back in the late 1960s.

TITCHMARSH MARINA

Prior to constructing the marina, Percy Titchmarsh and his son John built boats in premises in Mill Lane, just off the High Street. The old shed has long gone and in its place is a new development of houses now called Marina Mews.

Above the junction with the Twizzle Creek, the channel passed

ESSEX AND SUFFOLK BOATYARDS AND BOAT BUILDERS

Regd. in England No. 1027879   V.A.T. Regd. No. 103 3396 05

COLES LANE, WALTON-ON-NAZE, ESSEX CO14 8SL
Tel: Frinton-on-Sea (01255) 672185   Fax: Frinton-on-Sea (01255) 851901

Titchmarsh Marina

Foundry Creek to port and leads to the head of the creek where the first buildings found are Walton and Frinton Yacht Club, sited on the spot where a windmill used to operate. It is one of the earlier yacht clubs, being formed in 1908.

This small basin was created by the Club from a tidal pool in which were located various craft and houseboats. It was dredged out and a lowering gate fitted at the entrance. It is good facility to use if visiting Walton-on-the-Naze and the Yacht club will extend a warm welcome.

The creek splits here and to port, the quayside, run by Frank Halls & Sons is at the head of the tidal channel. Just passed the quay the remains of a water mill are just visible in the form of sluice gates, the pond being used for many years as a boating lake but for several years has been derelict. I remember one afternoon, taking time off from my studies at the Technical College in Colchester in 1959, driving in my 1935 Austin 7

Walton & Frinton Yacht Club Pool

accompanied by my current girlfriend, we hired a sailing dinghy on this boating lake.

The lake was very shallow and the dinghy had no centreplate with the consequence that she sailed well down wind but would not sail back to windward, so I had to row back.

Frank Halls & Sons

Frank Halls & Sons were established in 1920 by Frank Halls and Claude Brookes, then known as Brookes and Halls, building small rowing and sailing boats and the Gem class of which a large number were built for members of the Walton & Frinton Yacht Club. In the later 1920s they built a number of the 18' Walton One Design, some of which survive today. In the early 1930s Mr. Brookes left the firm to start an iron mongers and Frank Halls took his son Alf into the business and it became Frank Halls and Son. Frank died in 1934 and Alf carried on with yacht work until the outbreak of the Second World War when in 1940 the firm

FRANK HALLS & SON

Proprietors: D. N. Halls, J. L. Halls Established 1920
E. Halls, J. M. Halls

Office & Works: V.A.T. Reg. No. 102 2955 06

MILL LANE . WALTON-ON-NAZE . ESSEX . ENGLAND CO14 8PF

TELEPHONE:
FRINTON-ON-SEA
(STD CODE 025 56) 6596

Above: Frank Halls & Son • Below: Kestrel Class Yacht

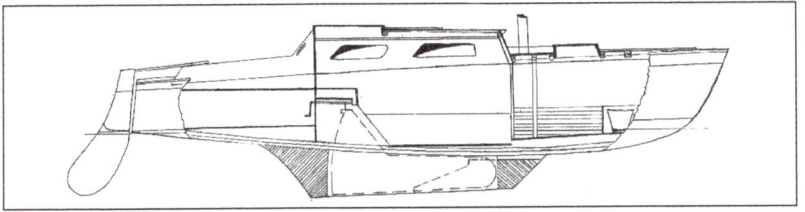

Tideway 25 being built

was closed and Alf served as a full time lifeboatman during the war. In 1945 he was joined by his son Derek and in 1955 his brother John joined the firm and they continued to build rowing and sailing dinghies. In 1959 they started to build the 22' Kestrel centreboard class, of which some 36 were built.

The price of this delightful centreboarder in 1960 was £725.00 and for an extra £175.00 you could have a 4hp Stuart Turner fitted.

This 25' Clinker Sloop was built in 1983 to a design by the late Peter Brown.

The tools shown are similar to those used for many years in boatyards all over the country.

Frank Halls also carried out refit

and repairs to wooden yachts and my father berthed his yachts with them over a period of thirty years. These included 'Lora' 43' schooner, 'Picannin' Robert Clark 39' Mystery Class, 'Incognito' a Peter Duck (then Lloyds +100A1) and his last yacht a Stella, 'Four Bells'.

I also used their facilities first with 'Sea Feather', 50 square meter, then a Folkboat 'Rodingen', a Cheverton Crusader and cold moulded 25' Gaff Cutter.

In the 1970s, Frank Halls built a series of glass fibre yachts, designed by Van de Stadt, the Trintella 111A and Victory 40, using hulls moulded by Tylers and completing them to a high standard with teak decks and mahogany interiors.

A powerful cruising yacht, with excellent accommodation and good sailing performance. I helped deliver one from Walton-on-the-Naze to Brighton Marina and we ran under full sail and spinnaker, on auto-

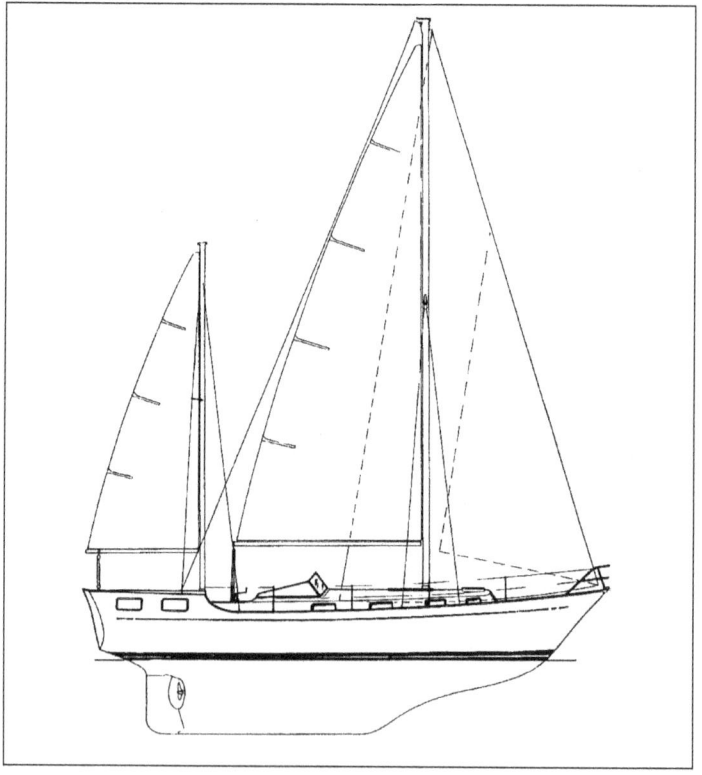

Trintella IIIA Ketch

pilot for several hours without having to make any adjustments.

In 1980 Frank's great grandsons Trevor and Christopher joined the firm, which they continue to run today.

Bedwell & Co

The small creek to the right of the Yacht Club leads up to Bedwell & Co, a yard established in the early 1960s.

The yard completed the fitting out of 'Sephine' a 37.8' auxiliary Yawl designed by J Francis Jones, who's hull was built by Frost & Drake at Tollesbury, in 1959. They carry out all types of refit work including rigging and engineering and have two covered slip sheds and winter laying up facilities. Started originally by Ron Wyatt, who has retired, the family still runs the yard today.

Bedwell & Co also had pontoon moorings in the Twizzle and it was here that I moored 'Timba' a Prior 30 built in strip plank in 1967 by R J

Bedwell & Co

Prior 30 'Timba'

Prior & Sons, Burnham-on-Crouch to a Chris Petrie design. She was the first one of several built and owned by Murray Prior for a while. A fin and skeg yacht with good performance. I bought her and refitted her totally in 1993, replacing half her decks and cockpit sole, removing and rebolting her skeg, new rigging, electrics, fuel and water tanks and more.

Ford Marine (Clacton) Ltd

Set up in the mid 1970s by Roy Dillon who produced the Duellist 32, designed by Alan Hill and moulded by Lifeline Moulding Co Ltd at Hoo, Kent. A shoal draft long keel yacht with lifting keel, ideally suited for coastal estuaries but also capable of offshore cruising.

FORD MARINE (CLACTON) LTD.
Ford Road, Clacton-on-Sea
Telephone: (0255) 23059

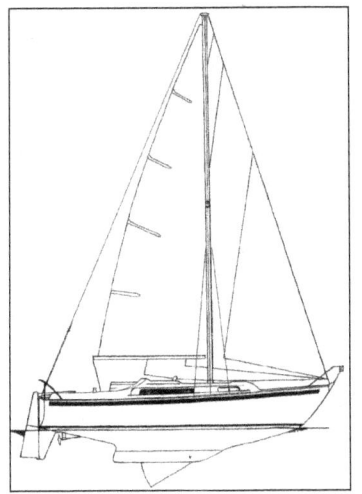

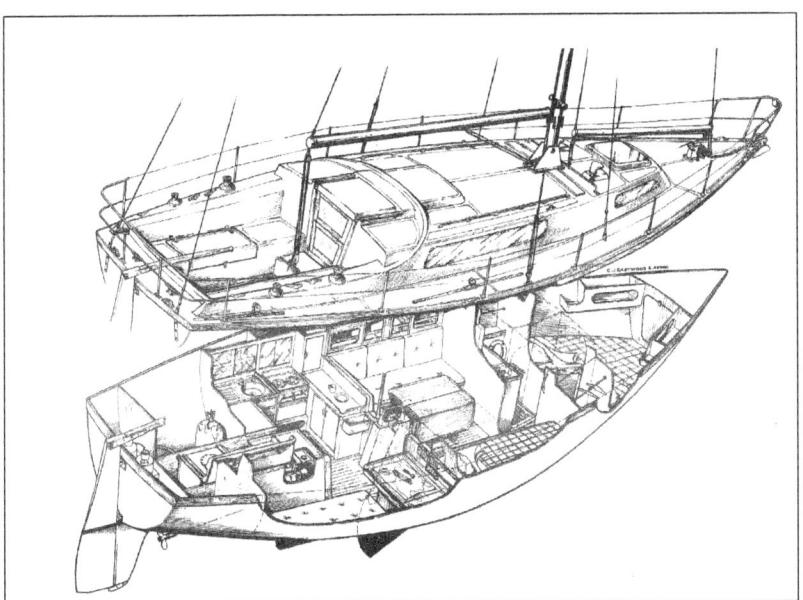

Duellist 32

CHAPTER 6

THE COLNE

SOME MILES WEST, ALONG THE Wallet, passing Walton-on-the-Naze and Clacton Piers, The River Colne runs for about eleven miles in a northerly direction, passing Brightlingsea to starboard and East Mersea to port. The Pyefleet creek branches off to port shortly after Mersea Stone and the main river continues past the entrance to Alresford Creek (starboard), onwards to Wivenhoe on the starboard bank, Rowhedge to port and finally Colchester.

Since Roman times the Colne has been a busy river, with ships trading to Brightlingsea, Wivenhoe, Rowhedge and Colchester, but most commercial traffic has now ceased and the river is used by yachtsmen and many restored Thames Barges and Fishing Smacks.

The Colchester Native Oyster is famous worldwide and Kerrisons still operate an oyster fishery based in Pyefleet creek, this tradition stretching back to when the Romans were here.

The old Anchor Hotel (now private apartments) at the top of the hard Colne Yacht Club building to the right

BRIGHTLINGSEA.

The Romans built a fort at Brightlingsea to protect ships entering the Colne for Colchester.

Ship and boat building has been carried on here for many years, starting with commercial vessel and later yachts.

Aldous Shipyard, Aldous & Son 'Cymbeline', 82 tons, 1863, 44.5' schooner.

Site of Aldous Shipyard – known today as the Shipyard Estate

Aldous & Rashbrook, 'Daisy' 1887, 24.6' cutter.
E Aldous, 'Mabel', 1866, 42.2' yawl.
C J Kidby, 'Freya', 1896 26.5 c/b sloop. 'Marguerite', 1887 22' cutter.
J R Kidby, 'Myrtle' c1879 29.6 cutter

James & Stone (builders of commercial and naval ships).

They also built some sailing dinghies, the Jewel, designed by Robert N Stone and the Brightlingsea One Design.

The Jewel was adopted by Walton and Frinton Yacht Club, where there are still some sailing today and by various other clubs.

Brightlingsea One Design

Designed by Robbie Stone in 1927 and adopted by the Brightlingsea Sailing Club the same year, the 18' Brightlingsea One Design is still sailing today. 'Jean' was the first one built by D Stone & Sons and they built the next 13, when in 1949 they became James & Stone and numbers 15 – 26 and 28 were built. T C White built number 27, 29 and 30 and 32 was built in 1990 by Malcolm Goodwin in Wivenhoe and various other builders, with a few more taking the known number to over 44.

'Gelasma'- Brightlingsea One Design racing at Wivenhoe 1987

New glass fibre BOD 'Grethe' 2007

Cyril White's premises

In 2006/7 a new glass fibre version was built by Petticrows of Burnham-on-Crouch. My brother Robin owned No 18 'Gelasma' and I bought her from him in 1987. The photo shows her during the Wivenhoe Regatta race from Brightlingsea to Wivenhoe in 1987.

WHITE & AUSTIN

Cyril White came to Brightlingsea in 1937 having attended Oundle School and completed an apprenticeship at Cammell Laird. He worked for Aldous who sent him to R J Priors at Burnham for a spell. Cyril then set up in old wooden buildings just off The Waterside with his partner Mr Austin. They built various wooden yachts including several Folkboats and some of John Leather's clinker gaff cutters. Cyril also did some work for my

Esther Lohse

> # JIM SPENCER : SAILING SERVICES
> SAILING INSTRUCTION - SKIPPERING SERVICES - DELIVERIES
> YACHTS & BOATS STORED, REPAIRED & REFITTED.
>
> Waterside Boatyard,
> 22, Waterside, Brightlingsea, Essex. CO7 0BB
> Telephone: Brightlingsea (0206 30) 2911
> VAT REG NO: 529 3098 28

brothers Robin and Anthony on their 3 masted gaff schooner 'Esthe Lohse' when she was being refitted and appeared in 'The Onedin Line', a BBC television series in the 1970s. Another first class shipwright, Tony Turl assisted Cyril at the time.

Cyril was to be seen sailing his Folkboat (without engine) in and out of Brightlingsea Creek well into old age. Towards the end, Jim Spencer took over the running of the yard and produced a pretty double ender in GRP.

One day, on one of my many visits, I saw Cyril (probably in his eighties) lying under a yacht, antifouling her. Her crawled out and stretched upright with a sigh or two and I asked him how he managed to do this at his age. "Well boy," he said. "The only advantage of being this old is that you can't feel some parts of your body."

On 24th April 2007 Cyril died aged 92 years and I was privileged to attend his funeral on May 3rd 2007 at All saints Church, Brightlingsea, where Jimmy Lawrence read a moving tribute to Cyril. We then drank a toast to him in celebration of his life at the Colne Yacht Club afterwards.

Cox Marine Ltd

In the old Aldous Shipyard Cox Marine built a variety of sailing and powered craft, mainly in GRP.

Originally set up by the Cox Brothers in Ipswich, building Piver designed trimarans in plywood and then GRP, they set up the yard in Brightlingsea in the 1970s and were joined by Captain Willem In't Veld who managed the business and developed it over the years until his tragic death in 1986 in a motorcycle accident.

Their range of craft ran from the Cox 21(one completed a transatlantic crossing in 1975), Cox 22 Ketch, Cox Master Mariner, Cox 27, Cox 12 metre. They also fitted out Colin Archer hulls in grp.

In the early 1980s Cox Marine also fitted out a number of Colin Archer 40s from hull mouldings supplied by the Colin Archer Club of

Cox Marine's premises now used by another company

Stockholm, Sweden. These were fitted out with various rigs and accommodation layout.

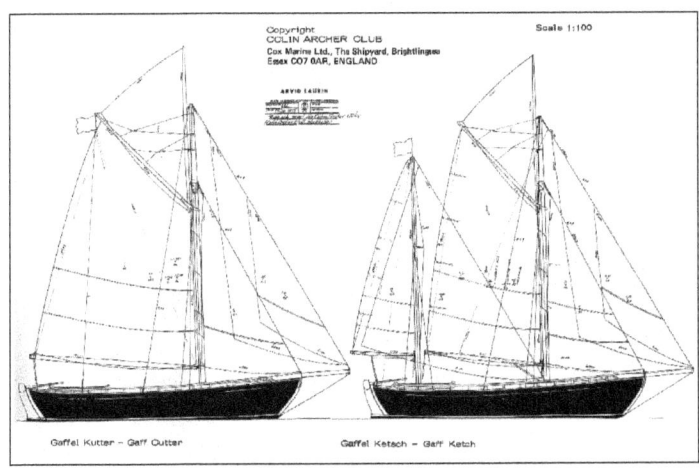

Colin Archer 40

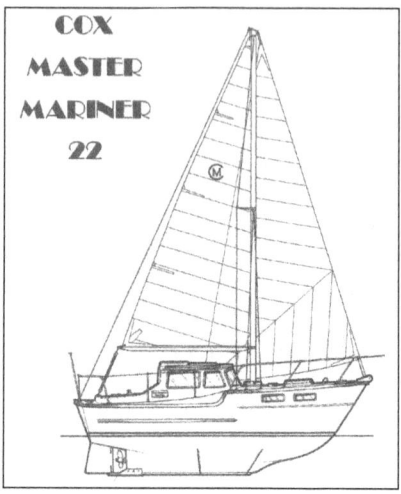

Cox 22 Mk 3   Cox22 Master Mariner

The company was bought by Irvine Martin (Plastics) around 1986 and yacht building declined and finally ceased in the late 1980s.

K. H. Marine

In premises in Lime Street, K H Marine produced the Swin Ranger, designed by Bill Scales, a boat builder next door. Available as a motor

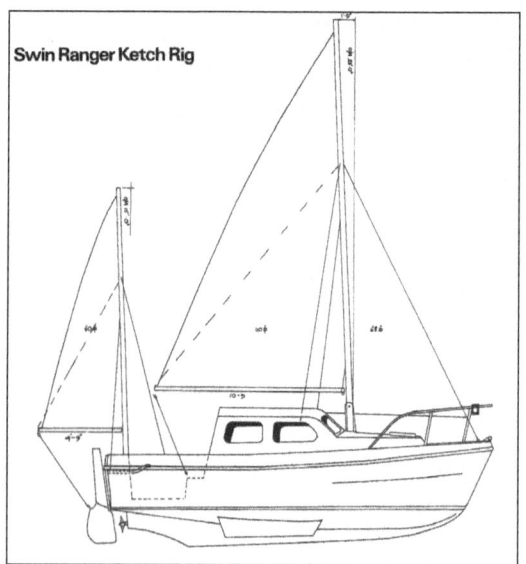

Swin Ranger Ketch

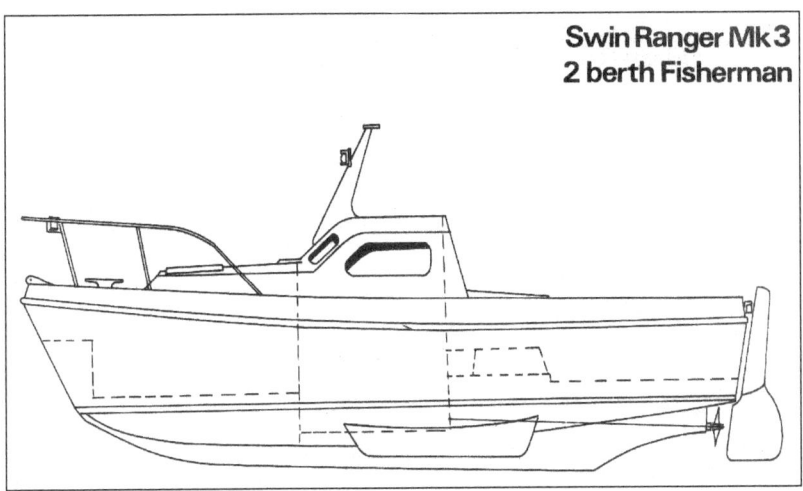

Swin Ranger Mk 3

cruiser or sloop or ketch rigged motorsailer, these were built in the late 1970s for a number of years.

Sailcraft Ltd

Reg White was building catamarans around 1960, designed by J R Macalpine-Downie. Three of these are shown here.

Reg White set up Sailcraft Ltd in 1967 and in conjunction with Rodney Marsh, designer, produced two Tornado catamarans, which raced in the IYRU trials. They were successful and were selected to be the 'B' class catamaran. Originally built in stressed plywood, the GRP version followed in foam sandwich construction, proving to be stiffer and lighter. Reg White campaigned the Tornado and with John Osborn they won the

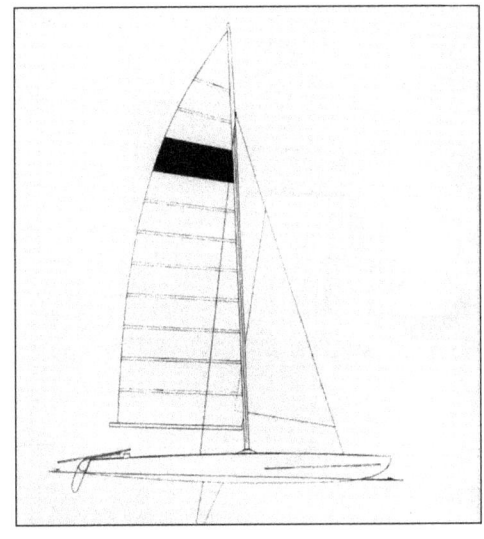

Hellcat Mk II – winner Catamaran International Challenge Cup off Long Island, New York 1960 and 1st outright at Thorpe Bay 1961

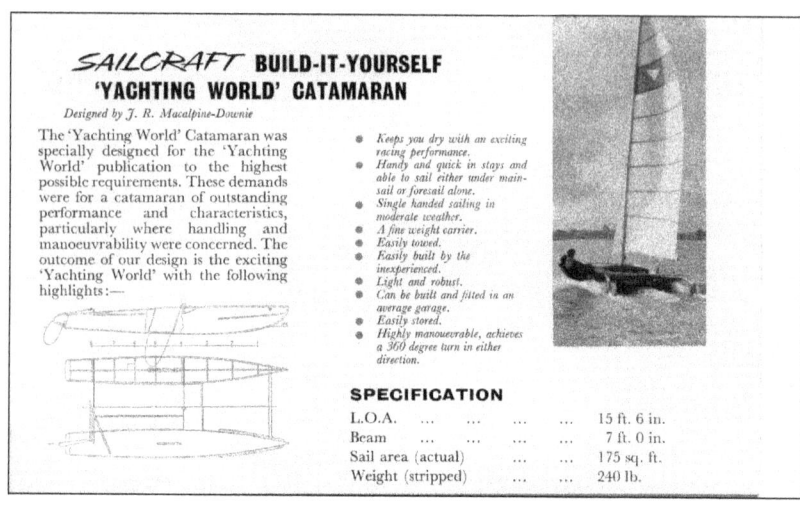

Yachting World catamaran

Olympic Gold Medal for the class in 1976. They were also building the Australis 'A' Class catamaran but production has ceased to concentrate on the Tornado. In 1973, recently returned from Australia, I arranged with Reg White to build the Australis and took the moulds to premises at Tendring. After constructing a new deck mould with special non-slip pattern moulded in, I produced about a dozen of these graceful craft.

Originally built in stressed plywood, these were now constructed in GRP with vacuum foam sandwich – each half of the hull and the deck are laid up with gel coat, glass cloth, resin and a layer of

Thai Mk IV – swept the board at Stokes Bay S.C. in 1960

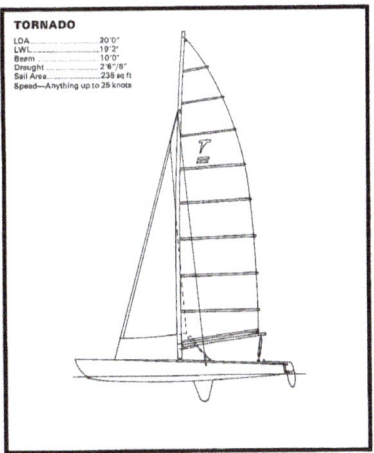

TORNADO
LOA .... 20'0"
LWL .... 19'2"
Beam .... 10'0"
Draught .... 2'6"/8"
Sail Area .... 236 sq ft
Speed—Anything up to 25 knots

polyurethane foam and placed in a rubber bag from which the air is extracted to minus two atmospheres and left to cure for a few hours. The hulls were then joined together and reinforcing areas (for beams, dagger boards etc) glassed in. Finally the deck was clamped down on a mix of resin and micro balloons. Hopefully, when opened up the next day, all was well. On the odd occasion it wasn't, with some built in flaw that rendered the hull/deck unit unusable.

Also being built in premises at Water Tank Road, in 1965 to a design by Rodney Macalpine-Downie, was the Iroquois Catamaran, originally in plywood and then in GRP. One of these early catamarans won the Crystal Trophy Round Britain Race. A graceful looking craft with good performance, the Mk I was followed by the Mk II and then Mk IIa which had two diesel engines placed right aft in each hull. This reduced the performance under sail.

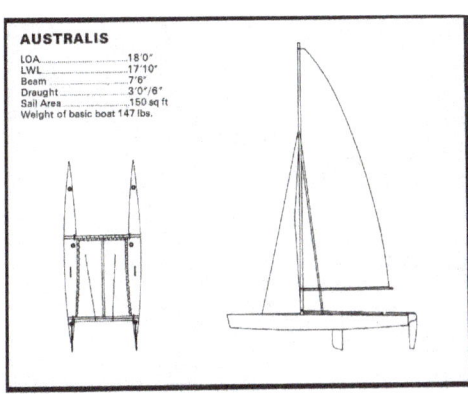

AUSTRALIS
LOA .... 18'0"
LWL .... 17'10"
Beam .... 7'6"
Draught .... 3'0"/6"
Sail Area .... 150 sq ft
Weight of basic boat 147 lbs.

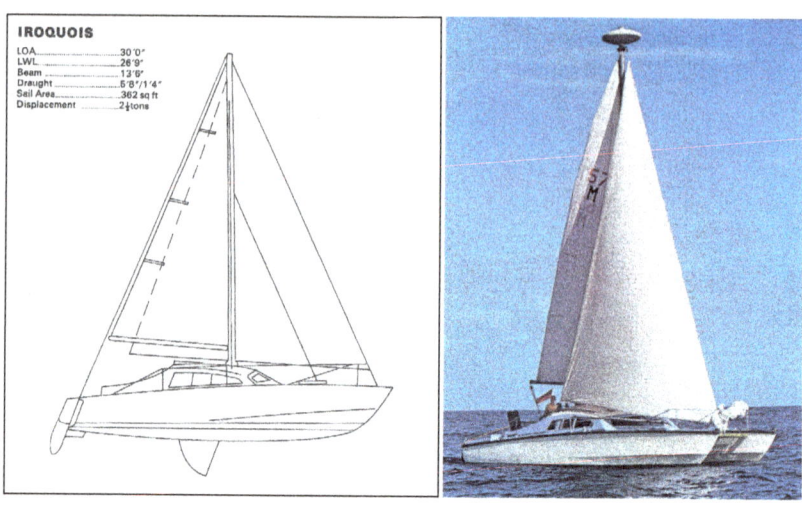

Iroquois Mk II Catamaran

In 1972 the Navaho was built – 46'LOA with a 20' beam, constructed in glass fibre balsa sandwich. Sailcraft went on to produce several more designs by Rodney Macalpine-Downie.

The Cherokee appeared in 1972 with its debut in 1973 at the London Boat Show. It was a large roomy cruising catamaran but still with a pleasing profile.

In 1973 the Apache was produced. Much larger at just over 40 feet but still unmistakably from the same designer.

1978 saw the appearance of the Comanche catamaran, smaller than the Apache.

In the mid 1980s Sailcraft sadly went into liquidation but in the 1990s Reg White set up building racing dinghies again, trading today as White Formula Ltd and operating from premises the Old Shipyard Estate. His son Robert is also in the business and they built a range of specialist racing dinghies including Taz, Topper, Topaz, Magno, Omega, Xenon, Vibe, BlazeX, Byte CII, SL 16, Spitfire, Shadow, Hurrican and Challenger.

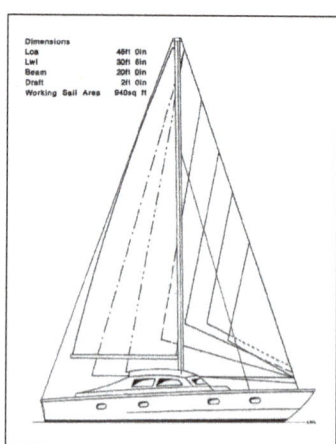

Sailcraft Navaho

 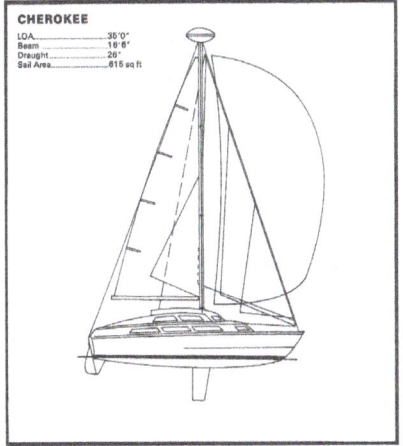

Above: Sailcraft Cherokee catamaran • Below: Sailcraft Apache catamaran

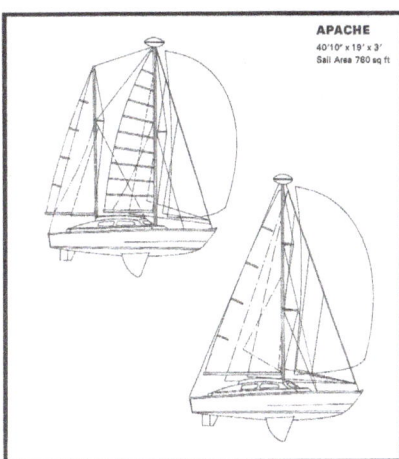 

COBRAMOULD (LEISURE YACHTS)

Appearing here is a company that started trading in Stansted, Essex, but moved to Brightlingsea around 1980 and changed their name.

Cobramould were building the Leisure range of yachts in premises near Stansted Airport and started with the Leisure 17, designed by Arthur Howard in 1966.

Yachting World produced a report on this little yacht in 1971, com-

Brinecraft Limited
Morses Lane Industrial Estate
Brightlingsea
Essex CO7 0SD
Telephone: Brightlingsea (020630) 2616

menting in very favourable terms. By this date some 540 had been built.

The Leisure 20 followed, with similar lines and bilge keels.

Designed by Graham Craddick the Leisure 22 appeared in 1971 again in either bilge keel or fin keel versions.

The next yacht, the Leisure 23, was designed by Frank Pryor and followed the format with either bilge keel or fin keel models available.

A much larger yacht was produced – the Leisure 27 which was a popular choice for family cruising.

Around 1980 the company moved to Brightlingsea with premises in Morse Lane and produced the Leisure 20, trading briefly as Leisure Yachts on their literature.

They changed their name to Brinecraft Marine Ltd and produced the SL range of Leisure

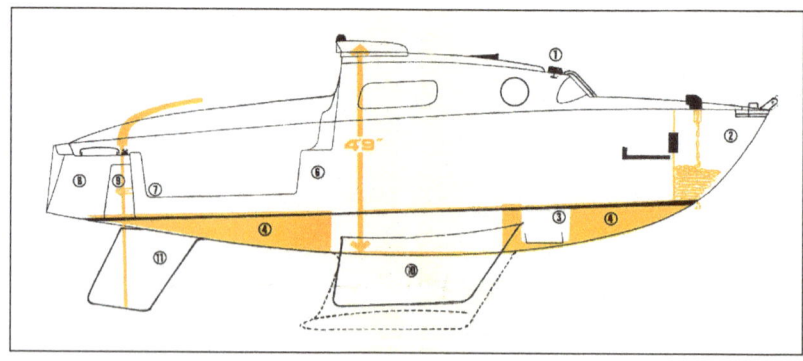

Leisure 17

Leisure 22

yachts, mainly with new deck mouldings, starting with the Leisure 17SL. The 23SL followed

Around 1984 Leisure Yachts produced the Leisure 26 Elite, based on the old Oyster 26. They also produced the Leisure 29, the largest yacht they built in the 1980s, which was identical inside to the Leisure 27 but redesigned from the companionway aft.

Leisure 20

Leisure 27

Leisure 17SL

Leisure 23SL

In 1990 the company experienced a disastrous fire and ceased trading – several items were later auctioned off in Ipswich.

Production moved to Germany for two years where new moulds were made for the 17SL and 23SL with assistance from Tom Winyard, owner of Brinecraft.

A small number of 17SLs were built Corfu and the moulds later returned to Germany.

Leisure 26 Elite

It is believed that the 17SL and 23SL moulds ended up in Poland.

Boating Scene (builders of the Mirage Yacht range) bought the Leisure name and built the 27SL, derived from the Mirage 27 around 1989.

St. Osyth Boatyard Ltd.
St. Osyth Nr. Colchester Essex
Telephone St. Osyth 820278

ST OSYTH BOATYARD

Located upstream from Brightlingsea at the top of St Osyth Creek, a drying creek where there used to be a water mill. The large lake that fed the mill remains above the road and the mill used to stand on the St Osyth village side of the road.

David Budworth owned the yard in the 1950s with Dennis Barnes running it later. The yard built some 22' Kestrels, an East Anglian and other yachts including in 1963, a 36 foot glass fibre yacht, designed by Camper & Nicholson, moulded by Halmatic and finished off by the yard to Lloyds +100A1 – they also carried out general repairs.

In the early 1962 they built the Peregrine class, designed by J Francis Jones, a reverse sheer lifting keel yacht of 27.75' LOA and a beam of 8.5', clinker built of mahogany, larch or wych elm with ply decks.

St Osyth Boatyard

Peregrine Sloop 'Jack o'Lantern'

Malcolm Vertigan took control in the early 1970s and carried on refit work and opened up a chandlery. Around 1973 it was purchased by local car auctioneers and the director at this time was Ronald Leader.

Dick & Andy Harman then bought the yard and they continue to operate it today carrying out general refit work on yachts, smacks and barges.

Wivenhoe

A few miles upstream from Brightlingsea, the pretty riverside village of Wivenhoe lies on the east bank.

MIKE DAVIES

Site of old dry dock – now an ornamental pond in the new housing development

Ship and boat building has been carried on here since early times.

Evidence of shipwrights date back to the early 1500s and in 1650 Robert Page built the small trading ketch 'Nonsuch'. In 1668-9 'Nonsuch' sailed to Hudson's Bay on a trading voyage that was to lead to forming of the Hudson's Bay Company. The Page family operated for four or five decades constructing cargo vessels and some naval craft. In 1654 they built 'Fagaris' a 348 tonner with 22 guns.

Eighteenth Century shipbuilders included William King and Austin Stanley was operating a shipyard upstream of the quay in 1734.

On salt marshes, formerly oyster layings, John Flack had a shipyard and was taken over by George Wyatt in 1757. Moses Game built ships for the government but was bankrupt in 1784.

Philip Sainty (1754-1844) was the main boat and yacht builder in the later 18th century and early 19th century with a yard upstream of the quay. He built many fishing smacks and schooners as well as the yacht 'Pearl' in 1820 for the Marquis of Anglesey and the frigate 'Pearl' in 1828.

William Hawkins, a Colchester timber merchant launched some ships from the same yard in the early 19th century. John Kidby was less fortunate and was bankrupt in 1841.

Thomas Harvey acquired the upstream yard on Sainty's bankruptcy in 1834 and he and then his son John became well known for their racing yachts.

They built fast schooners to bring fruit and other goods from Spain

New housing built on Wivenhoe Port site

and the eastern Mediterranean in exchange for fish. In 1874 he designed and built 'Sea Belle', 192 tons and 'Miranda' in 1876. Both vessels were crewed and captained by Wivenhoe men.

Wivenhoe reached its peak for yacht building in the 1870s before wood gave way to metal and it was overtaken by yards in the north.

In 1872 John Harvey's yard suffered a severe fire from which it did not fully recover. The yard was occupied from 1881 to 1888 by E.J. Wilkins and then taken over by Forrest & Sons Ltd from Limehouse, London, building in steel. They constructed the dry dock.

In 1912 G Rennie & Co of Greenwich joined with Forrest to become Rennie Forrest Shipbuilding, Engineering and Dry Dock Co Ltd. A decade of expansion followed when many ships were built for the British and foreign governments. They constructed a steam launch for Dr Livingstone for use on what is now Lake Malawi. In 1922 the firm was bankrupt.

Other shipbuilding firms who took over the yard between the wars were also unsuccessful.

During the Second World War, the upstream yard built wooden minesweepers and Vosper Ltd came up from Portsmouth to occupy a downstream site where it built motor torpedo boats. On another upstream site Dorman Long built a large part of the Mulberry Harbour used in the 1944 invasion of France.

I remember when the yard was still working in the mid 1950s, my brother and I would cycle from East Mersea to Rowhedge and take our bicycles over the ferry to Wivenhoe, cycle down Ferry Road (now engulfed in the new housing development) and stop at the top end of the yard where, in a mud berth, lay the 'Cap Pilar', a wooden sailing ship in which Adrian Seligman had circumnavigated the globe just before the war, with a crew of amateurs. She was an inspiring sight and our young minds conjured up all kinds of adventures she must have gone through. Later, she was moved into the dry dock and broken up.

I attended the final auction at the yard and one of the last lots was described as a "pile of firewood". The gentleman who made to winning bid went home and returned with a wheelbarrow and enquired where he could collect his 'firewood'. The auctioneer waved to the dry dock and said it was there, where upon the gentleman walked over and gazed down at the keel and other remaining timbers of the once fine ship 'Cap Pilar'.

The yard closed in 1962.

Between 1966 and 1981 the yard was occupied by J Gliksten & Co, a timber importing company. Whilst converting the Old Congregational Chapel adjacent to the yard, we purchased two standards of timber straight off the ship for use as floor joists.

Wivenhoe Port Ltd then used the site for grain storage.

In 1988 it was acquired by Property Associates Ltd for housing development. Today there are many new houses on the old shipyard site.

Believed site of Husk's Boatyard

Joseph Cole and his son Daniel built smacks from 1800-1820s at a yard believed to be downstream of the quay.

James Husk and his successors working in a yard downstream of the quay, built smacks and yachts from the 1840s until 1937. The photograph (2007) shows what is believed to be the site of Husk's boatyard, now part of the housing development going on at the premises and those of James Cook & Co.

Malcolm Goodwin's premises

Cox & King operated from a nearby yard in the early 20th century.

This yard area became the site developed by James Cook & Co who built a great variety of vessels from 1947, up to 2,000 tons. One of the last vessels built here was the 'Lord Nelson', a steel sailing vessel for the Jubilee Trust but due to the imminent closure of the yard it was launched and towed to Vosper at Portsmouth for completion. The yard closed in 1986. The yard has been sold for housing development.

Located just up from the old Cooks Shipyard in St John's Road are the premises Malcolm Goodwin, now retired, who started building boats in 1979, specializing in racing dinghies and sails for them.

Included in the racing dinghies he built were Hornets, Fireball and general purpose dinghies were the Colne Gaffer, Water Rat, Nutshell and Toad. He also built No 32 Brightlingsea One Design in 1990 and rebuilt several over the years.

Not only building dinghies, he also was a successful helmsman in Hornets, winning the World Championship in 1972, 1973, 1974, the National Championships in 1973 and 1974 and the European Championship in 1973 and 1979. In 1982 he won the World Championship again at Mudeford.

COLNE MARINE & YACHT CO LTD

In 1953 Guy Harding set up the Colne Marine & Yacht Co Ltd in the centre of the quayside. Prior to this, a company named Gibson Power Craft had been building small wooden motor boats fitted with Austin

Colne Marine & Yacht Co Ltd

petrol engines, in the Rosabelle shed, visible in the photograph by the trees, from the late 1940s to early 1950s. They were launched on a set of rails, which ran from the shed to the water's edge.

He built a number of yachts, including 'Ylva' a 24 ton yawl and 'Tomahawk' a 7 ton sloop and several others. The Rosabelle shed was used for yacht construction and launching was carried out on 'greasy ways'. Mud berths were available in front of the yard.

I completed the refit of my Folkboat 'Rodingen' here in 1982.

Guy Harding launched her with his hand-operated crane (see crane in photo).

'Rodingen' Folkboat just prior to relaunching at Colne Marine 1982

New homes constructed from Colne Marine's buildings

The yard ceased trading in 1990s and the buildings have been converted into fine waterside homes.

A well known resident of Wivenhoe, Louis Worsp (now deceased) ran a fleet of fishing trawlers under the name of North Sea Canners. He also built his own yacht on the quayside at Wivenhoe in 1950. She was a 35.3' x 11.5' x 6.4' cutter to a design by Dr W Radcliffe, carvel planked on steel frames and originally fitted with a Bergius petrol engine, later changed to a diesel engine. Her name was 'Maid of Wyven'

Maid of Wyven

Mr Worsp's son, John and I went to the same school and one weekend in the mid 1950s he invited me out on the boat. Our voyage, for that's what it was for a small boy, lay down the Colne and out across the Thames Estuary to the Barrow Deep Lightship.

On reaching the Lightship, we had to scramble up a net hanging over the side – no mean feat for small boys as there was a strong sea running which produced a large swell, causing the yacht to rise and fall alarmingly.

We were carrying essential supplies of fresh food and drink and also the mail.

After looking all over the Lightship we descended the net to re-board the yacht for our journey home to Wivenhoe. Quite an adventure compared with today's children's main activity of watching the television or playing a video games.

John took over the yacht later and ran her for many years, maintaining her in immaculate order.

Today there is no ship or yacht building in Wivenhoe but the legacy of those earlier years of large yacht construction is still visible in the names of several streets – Rosabelle Avenue named after the 600 ton steam yacht, Britannia Crescent after the Royal Yacht, skippered by Captain Albert Turner from Wivenhoe, 'Valfreda Way' after the 700 ton steam yacht 'Valfreyia' (probably a spelling mistake by the council naming department.) and Vanessa Drive after the 250 ton steam yacht 'Vanessa'.

THE NOTTAGE MARITIME INSTITUTE

Located on the quayside near the Rose & Crown public house, this unique establishment was founded in 1896 after a fund was left by Captain Charles G Nottage for the foundation of an institute at which local people could improve their navigation skills. It has grown over the years and now boasts a large library and museum of artifacts from around the local area, mainly related to ship and yacht building. A registered teaching establishment with the Royal Yachting Association it holds courses on all aspects of navigation, rope work, weather forecasting, dinghy building and much more. I have attended various courses here over the years. It is open to visitors during certain times in the summer months.

JOHN LEATHER

Opposite Wivenhoe is the village of Fingrinhoe with Ferry Road running down to the River Colne. John Leather moved here in 1935 as a

The Nottage Institute

teenager, working on a farm. He studied engineering and naval architecture at the Colchester Technical College and served and apprenticeship as a ship draughtsman at The Rowhedge Ironworks Company. Marrying Doris in 1955 they settled in Wivenhoe and John joined Lloyds Register of Shipping in London as a ship surveyor rising to senior surveyor at Southampton.

The family lived on the Isle of Wight for eight years before returning to Fingrinhoe in 1979. He had a lifelong interest in boats and small craft and designed many craft including the New Blossom gaff cutter, and other larger yachts and the Oyster, which is still built in Norfolk.

As a hobby he wrote 15 books, the first entitled Gaff Rig, which won Best Book of the Sea Award. He died at home in February 2006.

Rowhedge

Half a mile upstream from Wivenhoe on the west bank, lies the village of Rowhedge.

Ships have been built nearby at East Donyland since 1766. Samuel Spunner built ships at Rowhedge between 1803 and 1806. Oyster merchant and Wivenhoe shipwright Samuel Cook owned a shipyard and quay in Rowhedge in the late 1790s and passed it on to his nephew Daniel Cole.

Mr Harris has a workshop and wharf in 1808 and James Harris, boat

'Brightlingsea'

'Buttercup'

Merganser

builder was working in Rowhedge in 1841. In 1878 Peter Harris was a yacht and boat builder and in 1899 built 'Gossip', 41' gaff cutter with a Brooke petrol engine and the business continued by his son until taken over by Rowhedge Ironworks in 1916.

Susannah Cole owned a shipyard operated by William Cheek around 1839 in the north of the parish of Rowhedge.

There were various other people building yachts including the Ouxley family from 1878 and the Houston family by 1894. Some 60-70 men were employed here in 1898 until a fire burnet it down – it had become Donyland Shipyards by 1902.

In 1904 Walter Oxton, Frank Ernest Maslen and Lewis Penrose Foster, all on the staff of Swan Hunter & Wigham Richardson Ltd., purchased Donyland Shipyard Ltd. They started trading in 1904 and were incorporated as the Rowhedge Ironworks Co Ltd., on 22nd February 1905.

This yard built a great variety of craft ranging from steam launches, small tankers, tugs, dredgers, hopper barges and sternwheelers for the Nile.

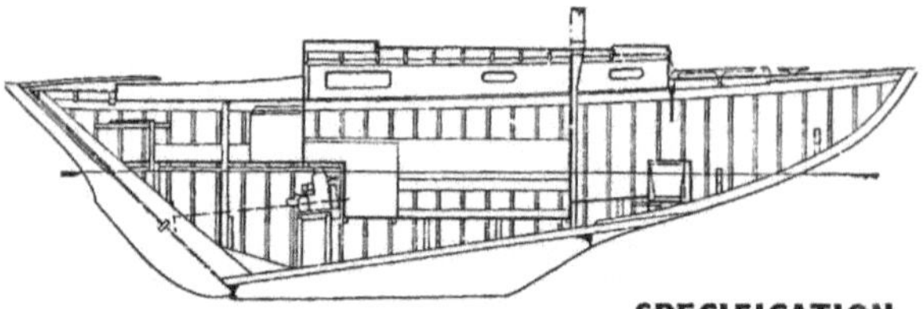

SPECIFICATION

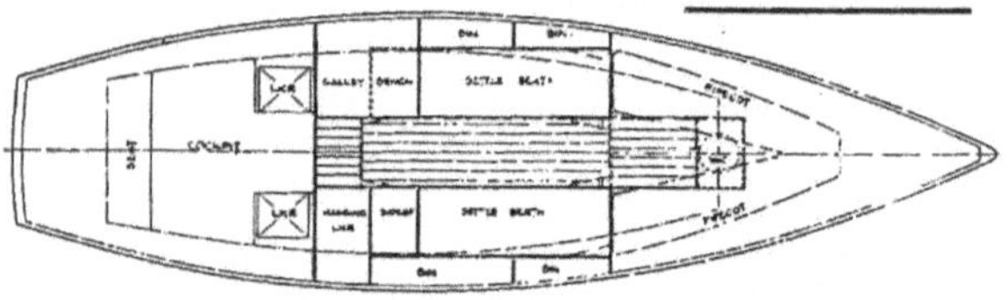

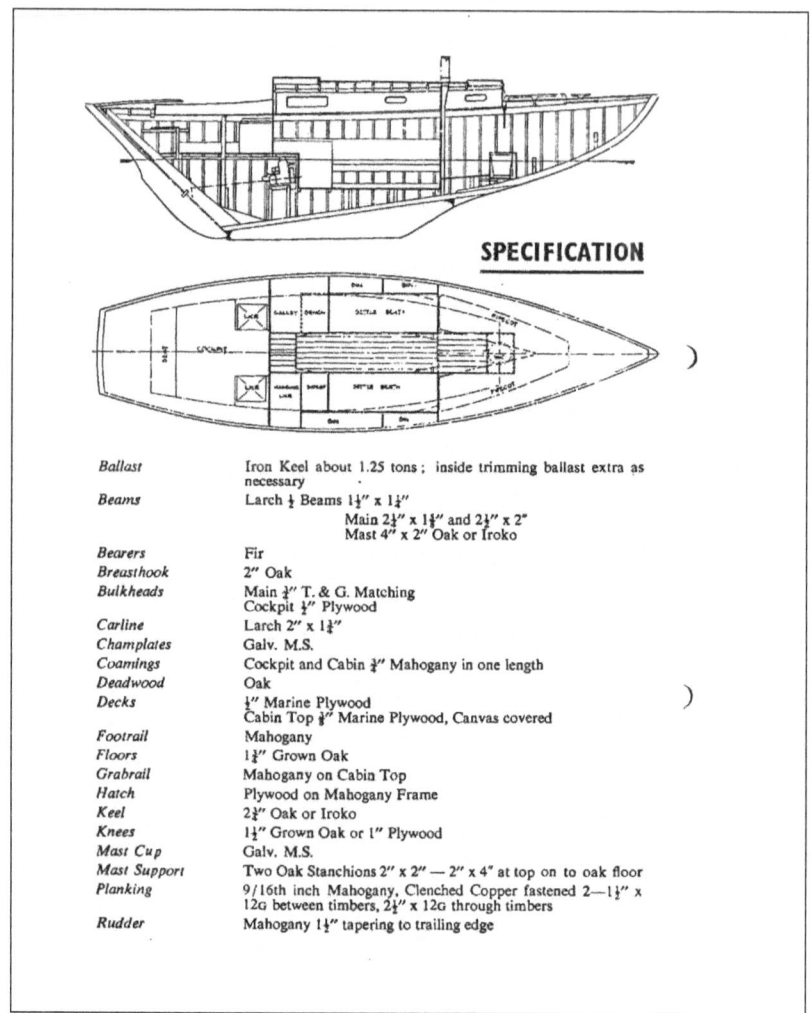

Ballast	Iron Keel about 1.25 tons ; inside trimming ballast extra as necessary
Beams	Larch ½ Beams 1½″ x 1¼″ Main 2¼″ x 1¾″ and 2½″ x 2″ Mast 4″ x 2″ Oak or Iroko
Bearers	Fir
Breasthook	2″ Oak
Bulkheads	Main ¾″ T. & G. Matching Cockpit ½″ Plywood
Carline	Larch 2″ x 1¾″
Champlates	Galv. M.S.
Coamings	Cockpit and Cabin ¾″ Mahogany in one length
Deadwood	Oak
Decks	½″ Marine Plywood Cabin Top ⅜″ Marine Plywood, Canvas covered
Footrail	Mahogany
Floors	1¾″ Grown Oak
Grabrail	Mahogany on Cabin Top
Hatch	Plywood on Mahogany Frame
Keel	2¾″ Oak or Iroko
Knees	1½″ Grown Oak or 1″ Plywood
Mast Cup	Galv. M.S.
Mast Support	Two Oak Stanchions 2″ x 2″ — 2″ x 4″ at top on to oak floor
Planking	9/16th inch Mahogany, Clenched Copper fastened 2—1½″ x 12G between timbers, 2½″ x 12G through timbers
Rudder	Mahogany 1½″ tapering to trailing edge

Stella Class One Design

In 1912, a special vessel was built in small sections, named Carolina and transported, partly by llama to Lake Titicaca the highest lake in the world at 12,500 feet in the Andes, Peru.

The 'Brightlingsea', a wooden ferry to carry 230 passengers was built in 1923 for London & N.E.Railway Company to operate from Harwich to Felixstowe.

The yard also built a number of yachts. In 1934 they built Starsong a 32.5' auxillary sloop designed by Capt. O.M.Watts and another of the same design, 'Stardrift' in 1937. 'Casquet', a 36' centerboard sloop designed by Arthur Robb in 1956 and 'Curtsey', 32.5' sloop by Alan Buchanan in 1962.

'Merganser' a 13 ton teak cutter was built in 1935, measuring 39' 4" and in 1936 'Buttercup' was built to a design by Robert Clark, 25' LOA with extreme curvature to the above water line areas – her planking was edge to edge requiring a high degree of workmanship. She had twin bilge keels and skeg, which allowed her to dry out upright.

Towards the end of their operations, Rowhedge Ironworks built a number of Stella Class sloops, designed by C.R.Holman – including these, Stella Lucia, 1960, Marie-Jon, 1961, Tishomingo,1961, Stella Mira,1963.

Rowhedge Ironworks finally closed in 1964 having built over 900 ships.

The upper yard became a general scrap yard and was sold in 1973. It has now been developed as a housing estate.

IAN BROWN LTD

Ian Brown took over the lower yard (Harris's) and ran it up to 1994.

He built several yachts including 'Celandine' a pretty 37' gaff ketch in 1967, designed by J Francis Jones, 'Odd Times' a solid 37.2' gaff cutter in 1968 to a design by John Leather and also serviced the RNLI lifeboats for many years.

With a covered slip and open slip he could haul out vessels up to around 100'.

My ex-wife's late father, Ray Donohoe, who came up to Wivenhoe from Portsmouth during the war and worked in the Wivenhoe Shipyard, moved to Ian Brown's in the early 1960s working as a shipwright.

Ian Brown's house still stands but the yard area has now been cleared and a housing estate built.

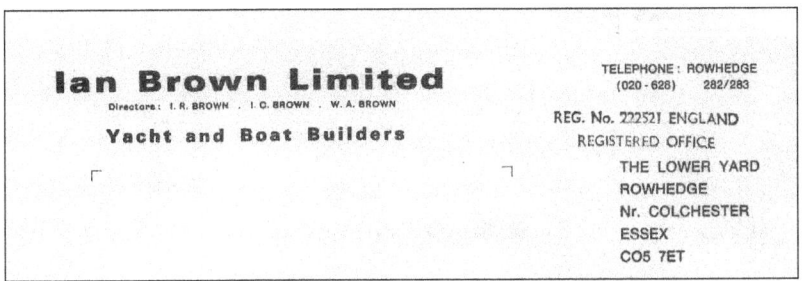

Ian Brown's house and yard site – now a housing development

Colchester

Upstream, some two miles, lies the port of Colchester.

The Romans established the town as a major centre and undoubtedly brought goods up the river, probably unloading at Rowhedge or Wivenhoe.

As far back as 1341 there was a landing at the Hythe or New Hythe.

Records show a footbridge was built in 1407, replaced by a cart bridge in 1473-4.

Shipbuilding was carried on at the Hythe from 1779-1822, mainly smacks, sloops, cutters and yawls of between 10-25 tons burden. In 1790 the Colchester yard built 13 ships. William Stuttle built ships at the Hythe from 1790, the yard passing on to Westerby Stuttle by 1818 and may have been acquired soon afterwards by Philip Sainty who built ships at Colchester from around 1819 to 1848 or so.

The Port of Colchester was finally closed by Act of Parliament in 2001 after some 2,000 years of commercial use.

Tamarisk 19

A company building glass fibre yachts in Colchester is North Sea Craft Ltd at Commerce Way, just up from the Hythe.

North Sea Craft Ltd originally was established in the early 1980s, then based in Norwich and built the Tamarisk 22 and Tamarisk 24.

The current company is run by David Cannel, the designer and Richard Swinton, who builds the Tamarisk 19, a delightful traditional shaped centreboard gaff sloop, and another of David Cannell's design, the North Sea 127. This is a powerful ketch based on the Colin Archer shape of pilot cutters and rescue yachts from Norway many years ago.

Oyster Marine also has a glass fibre unit at the rear of the quayside.

North Sea 127

CHAPTER 7

THE BLACKWATER ESTUARY

ONE OF THE LARGEST ESTUARIES on the East Coast, the Blackwater Estuary contains several creeks. It can be approached from The Wallet (from north) or The Spitway (from the South - also through the Ray Sand Channel).

WEST MERSEA
Just inside the entrance of this wide estuary lies West Mersea, entered by leaving the Nass Beacon to port and picking up port and starboard hand buoys laid by West Mersea Yacht Club.

Two main boatyards were in operation here, one William Wyatts and the other Clarke & Carter.

WILLIAM WYATT LTD
William Wyatt, known as 'Admiral' served an apprenticeship as a shipwright at the Wivenhoe yard of John Harvey Ship & Boat Builder

Moiya 10' lugsail dinghy after total refit

Company and was building in the early 1900s and carried out repairs and refits. William Wyatt joined his father in the small business repairing smacks and small fishing boats in a little weatherboard boatshed, which stood where the current Dabchicks Sailing Club clubhouse is built. The current yard is back along the road.

In 1989 I purchased a 10' dinghy from the Wilkins family of Tip-

Wyatts Boatyard

tree. She was built in the 1930s by William Wyatt as depicted on the brass plaque on her transom. The name on her transom when I purchased her was 'Genesta' and Mrs Wilkin told me that she was the tender to their yacht 'Genesta'. When I was restoring the dinghy I removed the name letters to reveal the name 'Moiya' carved in the centre of the transom – this I called her as it is believed superstitious to re-name a boat.

Some of the yachts built in later years included the following.

In 1954 'Merlander', 32' sloop was built to a design by J Francis Jones. A John Sloggett design named 'Eridani II' was built in 1957 and several Alan Buchanan and C Holman designs were built during the 1960s. In 1967 they fitted out a GRP yacht named 'Maverick' to a design by Holman & Pye and fitted out further GRP yachts as this material took over from wood in the late 1960s and early 1970s. The yard was later run by the late Harold Cutts and his wife Polly with boat builder Jack Emeny and today the premises are managed by Simon Cutts.

Gowen Sailmakers

Next to the current yard is Gowen Sailmakers, started by A A Gowen originally in Tollesbury and moved to West Mersea in 1919. His son Ken Gowen carried on the business, being joined by Paddy Hare in 1950 and then Colin Anstey. After a short period working under the Oyster Marine banner, the sailmakers are back under their own flag.

Gowen Sailmakers

ESSEX AND SUFFOLK BOATYARDS AND BOAT BUILDERS

CLARKE and CARTER Limited
STATEMENT
WEST MERSEA COLCHESTER ESSEX CO5 8NB   Telephone: West Mersea 382244

PETER B CLARKE
SHIPWRIGHT - MOORINGS - STORAGE - CHANDLERY
THE BOATYARD, 128 COAST ROAD, WEST MERSEA, COLCHESTER CO5 8PE
TEL/FAX: Yard (01206) 385905
Vat Reg.No. 368 6108 35

CLARKE AND CARTER LTD

Further up the road, Clarke and Carter's yard (on the original site of the Hempstead family boatyard) built occasional yachts but specialised in first class spar making. They also built up a large laying up area in front of the Victory Pub. The yard changed hands when the Barry and Nick Griffin took it over in the early 1970s and later still it was acquired by David Chatterton.

Currently the buildings are used by a variety of businesses.

Peter Clark owns the slipway in front of the yard and carries out general yacht repairs and hauling out.

Present buildings of Clarke & Carters

Slipway in front of Clarke & Carters

Mention must also be made of the well known yacht designers, Holman & Pye.

Started in 1956 by Kim Holman, a Cornishman who had worked for two years in Woodbridge with J Francis Jones. In 1960 Donald Pye joined the firm that became Holman & Pye. David Cooper joined the business and runs it today. Over the years they have designed some famous yachts, including the Twister range, the Stella class and large offshore yachts like Fanfare and Whirlwind.

JOHN MILGATE

Up the top end of the Ray Channel and almost hidden from view is located a delightful small boat business run by John Milgate.

He specialises in laying up and general refit work of traditional yachts and smacks. John served his time at Wyatts, West Mersea from 1945, when he went into the REME for

Smack 'Puritan'

John Millgate's premises

John Milgate with a current punt

National Service. After the war he returned to Wyatts and then joined the London River Police where he spent 13 years from 1956-1969. A short spell back at Wyatts after which he set up his own business in 1970 which he continues to run today at Peldon.

When I called on him in October 2007 he was continuing with the building of the smack 'Puritan' (originally dug out of the mud at Mersea) and some ply planked duck punts based on a design by William Wyatt circa 1916.

Tollesbury

Retracing one's route back down the Ray Channel and out to the Nass beacon where, turning to starboard brings one in to the Tollesbury Fleet, a north and south channel. Taking the south channel leads up to Tollesbury – the last part of the creek drying at low tide.

Tollesbury has been famous for oyster dredging – as far back as 1377 John De Heerde of Salcott was recorded dredging oysters.

Smacks were built here from the late 1700s. Tollesbury also supplied the crews and skippers of large yachts in common with men from the Colne.

Drake Brothers built a number of Thames Estuary One Designs to F Morgan Jones design in 1900 and in 1902 Tollesbury Yacht Berthing Company was formed to handle yachts now up to 300 tons, laying up in creeks and saltings.

It is interesting to note that the 'Crab & Winkle' Railway Line, opened around 1904, extended to the Pier when it was built in 1907. This was discarded in 1921, probably due to the decline in the oyster trade. In 1940 the pier was removed but I remember a small section of it was still there in the late 1950s when we sailed up the Blackwater. In 1952 the 'Crab & Winkle' line finally closed.

In 1924 Tollesbury Yacht & Boatbuilding Company was formed by Frost and Drake families. Drake Brothers still continued at the lower boatyard by the hard.

At this time Major McMullen had acquired an interest in the newly formed company and designed small cruising yachts, assisted in their building by Alfred Drake senior and his sons, Tom Frost senior and his sons – this work carrying on in what was formerly known as Gowen's sailmakers shop and loft at Woodrolfe Road. This was later used by CB Boats who built glass fibre power craft.

The business moved down the road to the saltings and Bontings Creek and is known today as Frost & Drakes boatyard. The premises are owned by Tollesbury Yacht Berthing Company, which is part of the Fellowship Afloat charity organisation.

FROST & DRAKE (Yachts & Boats) LTD
WOODROLFE ROAD
TOLLESBURY
MALDON ESSEX CM9 8SE
Telephone: 01621 869220

In 1949 Frost & Drake built the Harwich Bawley 'Jacqueline', 35' on deck. Built originally as a motor fishing boat she was converted to sail in 1991.

Frost & Drake

Mouse (Trevor) Green

Almost opposite Frost & Drakes yard is another boat builder, Mouse (Trevor) Green, who refits yachts in his yard and shed.

Mouse started in 1960 at Frost & Drake, serving an apprenticeship. From 1973 he worked at Tollesbury Marina for about seven years and in 1980 moved into the boatshed he works from today. This building was originally on another site and used by Cranfield and Carter, sailmakers. Mouse Green owns the Frost & Drake Company.

Mouse Green's shed

Tollesbury Marina

In 1969, on the old site of Drake Brothers old shipyard a new yachting centre was built by the late John Goldie and colleague Jack Waterhouse, by excavating the marshes to form a marina pool with sill.

Known originally as The Yacht Harbour and now Tollesbury

Tollesbury Marina

WOODROLFE BOATYARD

**The Yacht Harbour,
Tollesbury, Maldon, Essex, CM9 8SE
Telephone: (0621) 869202/868471**

Marina, it is administered by Woodrolfe Boatyard Ltd. The business is run today by Julian Goldie.

Also on the site is the Tollesbury Cruising Club.

A group of interesting buildings, known as the Sail Lofts are located on the left in Woodrolfe Road just before Frost & Drake's boatyard. Acquired in 1904 by Tollesbury Yacht Berthing Company and used for storage of yacht gear and later as various other businesses.

One of these businesses was Tollesbury International Marine set up in the early 1980s by Mervyn Rutter, dealing in brokerage yachts and new yachts from Vindo in Sweden.

Another sailmaker of note set up in Tollesbury in the 1970s, Gayle Heard (now deceased) who made yacht sails and was also involved in land yachting.

ESSEX AND SUFFOLK BOATYARDS AND BOAT BUILDERS

Sail lofts in Woodrolfe Road

A later picture taken in October 2007

MIKE DAVIES

COLVIC CRAFT

A little way inland at Witham used to be one of the most prolific moulders of modern glass fibre boats. Colvic Craft was established in the late 1960s by Colin Burns and Vic Pascoe. Their first premises were in Ardleigh and they traded under the title Ardleigh Laminated Plastics.

I recall visiting them there and saw both directors laminating one of their first craft, a 19'6" open launch which was supplied also with a deck moulding and wheelhouse.

They moved to larger premises at Witham and produced a large number of yachts and motorsailers, some from earlier manufacturers who had ceased trading, mainly as hull and deck units, with engines fitted. Photographs and drawings of some are shown following and the range included the Falcon 17, Colvic 20 Sailer, 24' Springtide, Colvic 23 Motor Sailer, Colvic Salty Dog 27, Colvic 29'6" Sailer, Colvic Atlanta 28, Colvic Sea Rover 28, Colvic Countess 33, Colvic Countess

Colvic Salty Pup 23

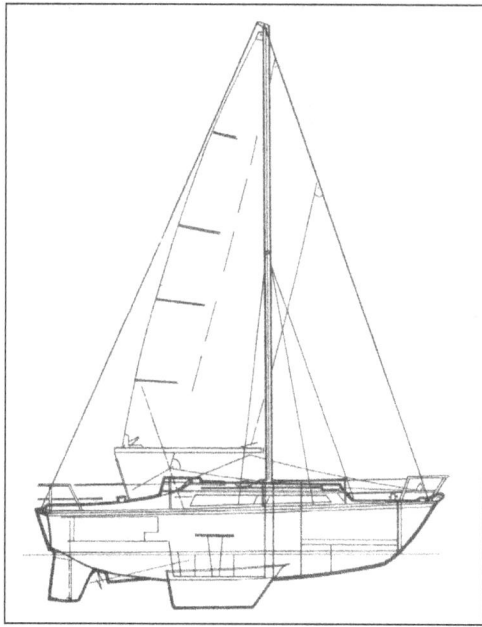

Colvic Sailer 26

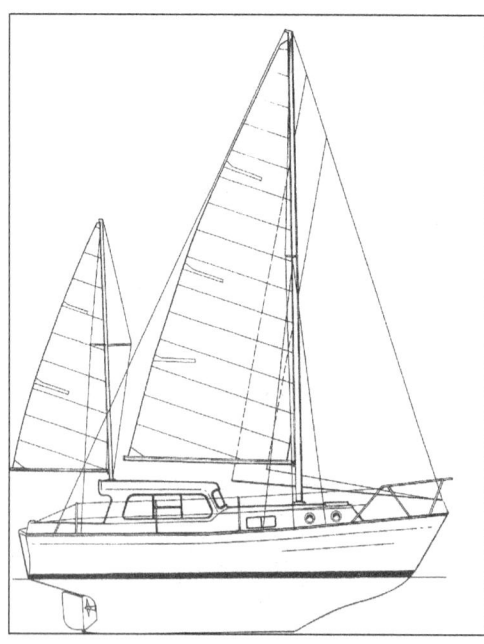

Colvic 31 Motor Sailer

35, Colvic Countess 37, UFO 31, UFO 34, Liberator 35, Victor Ketch range - Victor 34, Victor 35, Victor 40, Victor 41, Victor 50, the Watson Motor Sailer range - Watson 19' 6", Watson 23' 6", Watson 25' 6", Watson 28' 6" Watson 31' 6", Watson 34' 6", Majestic 48, 58/60, Bluewater 476, Bluewater 50-60. In their later years they constructed the eight 60' Round the World Racing Fleet for Robin Knox Johnson by which time they were located at Earls Colne, Essex.

Colvic Craft also produced several motor cruisers, namely 20' Seaskate, 20' Family Cruiser, 20' launch, 21' Searider, 22' Seaworker, 23' Seakeeper, 24, Canal Cruiser, 26' 6" Motor Cruiser, 28' Fast Angler, 28' Family Cruiser, 28' Motor Cruiser, 32' Coastworker, 29' Sunquest, 34' Sun Cruiser, 36' Sunquest, 40' Sunquest, 43' Sunquest, 44' Sunquest, 38' Trawler Yacht. Some are shown here.

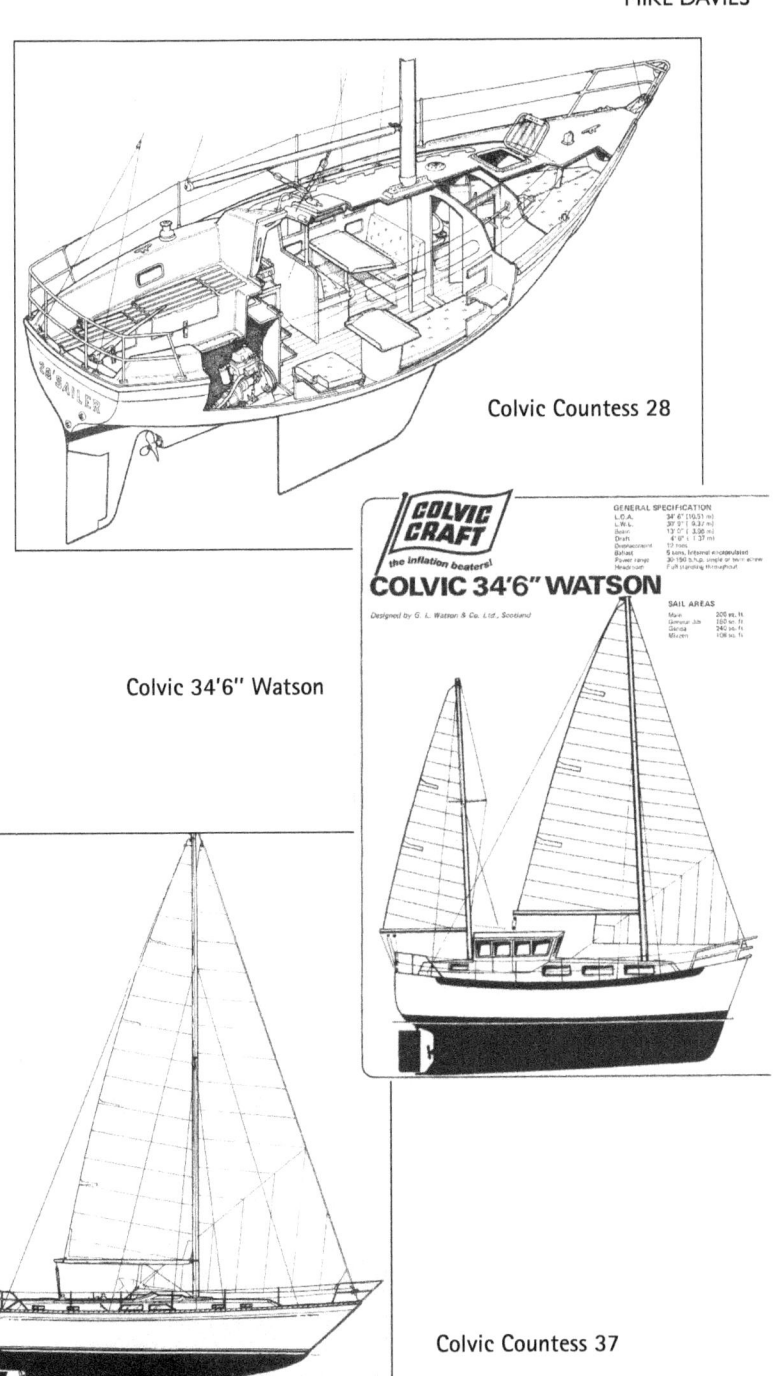

Colvic Countess 28

Colvic 34'6" Watson

Colvic Countess 37

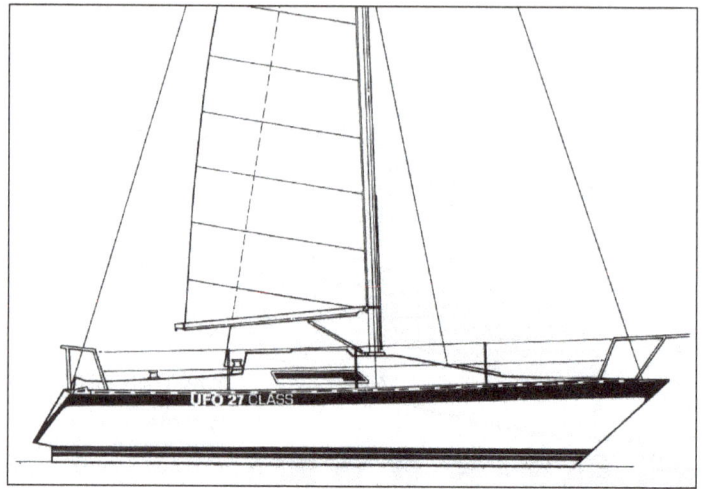

Colvic UFO 27

Colvic Victor 34

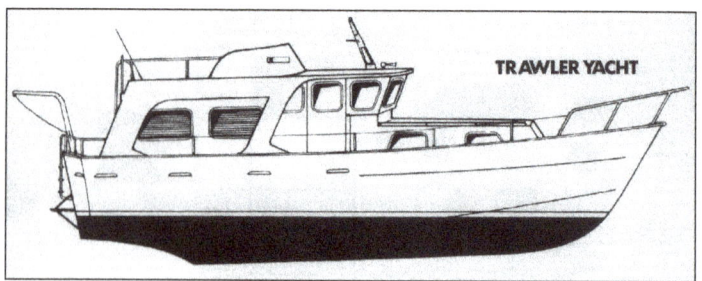

Colvic 38' Trawler Yacht

MIKE DAVIES

Above: Colvic Bluewater 476 • Below

Colvic 38 Trawler

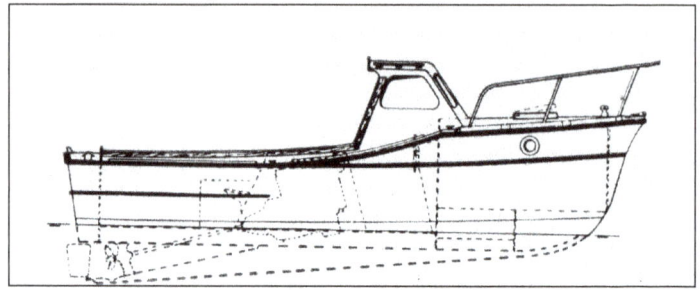

Colvic Seaworker 22

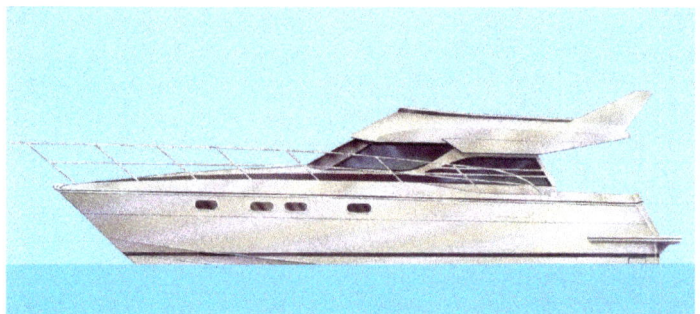

Colvic 44' Sunquest

Colvic 26' 6" Motor cruiser

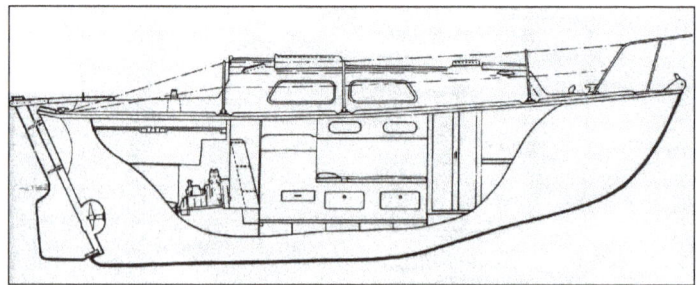

Colvic Springtide 24

SEAMASTER

A little further inland at Great Dunmow was located on of the earliest glass fibre boat builders. Established in the mid 1950s, Seamaster produced a large range of motor cruisers and yachts until their closure in 1981.

Taking the motor cruisers first they produced the following between 1958 and 1975. Seamaster 17 Cub, 17 Open, 20' Captain, 21', 24' Cadet, 25' Admiral, 26' Commander (from 1958), 27', 28' Commodore. Below are some illustrations of other motor cruisers.

Seamaster 23 (1968–1975)

Seamaster 725 (1980–1981)

Seamaster 8m (1970-1980)

Seamaster 813 (1972-1981)

Seamaster 820

Seamaster 30 (introduced at 1970 Boat Show – 1981, then as Norther 30 from 1984 under new Seamaster Company)

Other motor cruisers included the Seamaster 950 (1977-1981), the Seamaster 34 (1967 six built and more by other boatyards), Seamaster 1123 (1975-1976).

The yacht range consisted of the Seamaster 19 c1970 designed by Laurent Giles and those illustrated here.

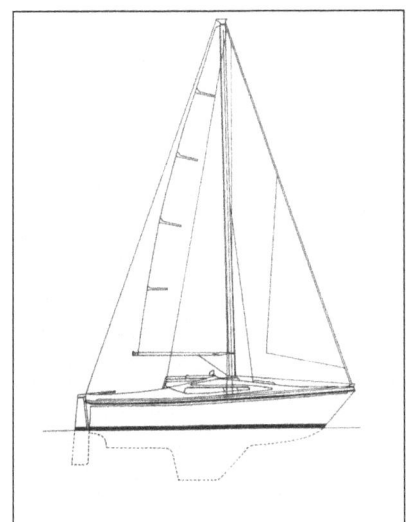

Seamaster 815 (1975- 1981 designed by Holman & Pye)

Seamaster 23 (1969-1975 designed by Laurent Giles & Partners)

Seamaster 925 (also known as 28 and 880, built from 1972 – designed by Holman & Pye)

Seamaster 29 (1979-1981 designed by Holman & Pye – Bounty Boats at Reedham, Norfolk continued to build these after 1981)

Bradwell Marina

MIKE DAVIES

M.A.M. (MARINAS) LTD.,
BRADWELL MARINA, WATERSIDE,
BRADWELL-ON-SEA, near SOUTHMINSTER, ESSEX
Telephone: Maldon 76235

BRADWELL-ON-SEA
On the south side of the River Blackwater and near the entrance, lies the village of Bradwell-on Sea. Bradwell has been easily located from seawards since the 1960s by the imposing grey monolithic buildings of Bradwell Power Station, one of the first atomic power stations to be built and now closed down.

The remains of a quay are still evident in the mouth of Bradwell Creek where barges used to load and unload their cargoes.

A MEMBER OF THE TASK TEAM GROUP OF COMPANIES

PORT FLAIR LTD.

BRADWELL MARINA, WATERSIDE, BRADWELL-ON-SEA, ESSEX CM0 7RB.
TEL: MALDON (0621) 76235/76391
COMPANY REGISTERED IN ENGLAND No. 1785526

BRADWELL MARINA
Just upstream from the old quay is the entrance to Bradwell Marina, established in the early 1970s by MAM Ltd (Music and Management) a company involved in the popular music business.

Excavated from the marshes at the edge of the creek, the marina gradually developed over the years with workshops and clubhouse.

In the mid 1980s it was purchased by Arthur Thurtle, Port Flair Ltd and continues in operation today.

Another company at Bradwell was JuxtaMare Marine who produced a quarter tonner named Listang in the late 1960s and 1970s, designed by Karl & Klaus Feltz. 24' 8" LOA with beam of 8' 2" and displacement of 2646lbs.

Like many quarter tonners this was of a fairly unique and easily

JUXTAMARE MARINE
QUAY WORKS
BURNHAM-ON-CROUCH
ESSEX
TELEPHONE:
BURNHAM-ON-CROUCH 3167.

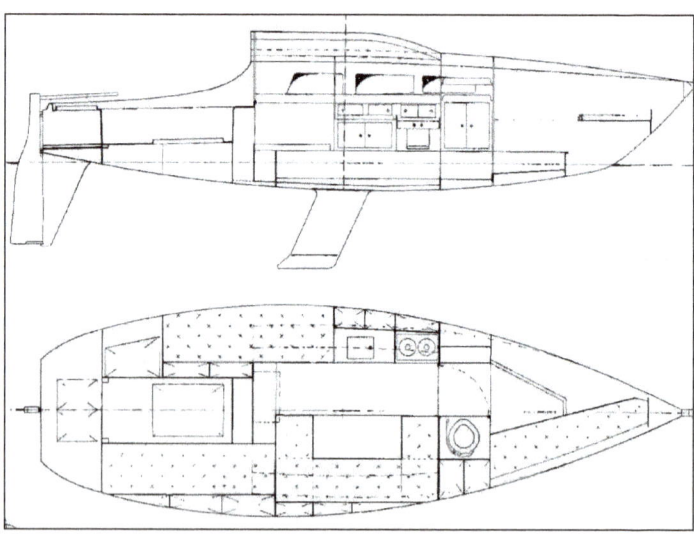

Listang

recognised shape.

It was a successful yacht and was 1st in Quarter Ton Cup 1969, 3rd in the Half Ton Cup 1970. 1st Class IV Buckley Goblets 1970 and 1st Mary Cup 1970. It was available in fin or lifting keel configurations.

Lawling Creek

Cardnell Bros

Almost opposite Osea Island on the south bank, Lawling creek runs up to Maylandsea where Cardnell Bros ran a large yard for many years, starting as G E Cardnell in the 1920s and listed as being in Steeple where he designed and built a number of yachts, amongst them being some pretty 20.8' yawls with canoe sterns – Arklight II was one of them. During the Second World War Cardnells built a number of craft for the Admiralty including eight 'B' class Fairmile Motor launches of 122 feet, used for patrol and anti-submarine work and other tasks. They also built some MFVs and 'D' class Fairmile 115 foot Motor Torpedo Boats. After the war the yard built a number of yachts, 'Matawa' 37.8' designed by F Morgan Giles and built in plywood (experience had been gained from war time construction using plywood), the Vertue, 'Grenade' to L Giles design in 1962 and many more.

In 1978 the yard was taken over by John Swinton of Swinton and Wilkingson, a timber business who had also taken over Dan Webb &

Cardnells Yard, now known as Blackwater Marina

Blackwater 38 Trawler Yacht

Feesey at Maldon. In addition to the land based business they also leased one and a quarter miles of moorings in Lawling Creek from Maldon Distric Council. It is now in new hands and named Blackwater Marina.

During John Swinton's ownership the yard imported from Taiwan and marketed three Trawler Yachts, the Blackwater 38, Blackwater 44 and Blackwater 48.

Located at Lower Mayland during the late 1960s and 1970s was Mayland Marine.

They produced a range of rowing/outboard dinghies, Fishing/

Blackwater 44 Trawler Yacht

DAN WEBB & FEESEY	THE SHIPYARD
YACHT BUILDERS · CHANDLERS · BERTHING & MARINE ENGINEERS	MARINE PARADE
(SWINTON & WILKINSON LTD.)	MAYLANDSEA · ESSEX · CM3 6AN
	TEL.: MALDON (0621) 740264 & 741267
	SHIPWAYS
	NORTH STREET
	MALDON · ESSEX · CM9 7HN
	TEL.: MALDON (0621) 54280 & 56829

Family Sixteen

Fisherman Sixteen

Camping cruiser and Family Sixteen and Fisherman Sixteen.

The river continues up past Osea Island, once a home for recovering alcoholics and used in the First World War years by the navy as a base for motor torpedo boats and minelayers.

Off the island, years ago, trading ships would unload their cargoes into barges for shipment to Heybridge Basin and beyond. I remember in the late 1950s we would sail into Heybridge Basin and after a meal we kids would roam about on the old barges lying in the basin, stacked with

STEEPLE ROAD   LOWER MAYLAND   ESSEX   CM3 6BE
Telephone: Maldon (Essex) 740518

TRIDENT LAMINATES LTD
112 THE CAUSEWAY
MALDON, ESSEX
ENGLAND
Tel. MALDON (0621) 55604

wood from the ships from which it had been unloaded.

FERGUSON BROTHERS (BRADWELL) LTD

Starting off in Southminster in the early 1970s, P.E.Ferguson designed and built the Bradwell 18, a practical lifting keel Bermudian sloop. The company moved to Heybridge Basin then to Maldon and continued to build these craft changing their name to Trident Laminates Ltd.

Paul Ferguson also designed the Bradwell 28, a centreboard, centre cockpit ketch with 9'4" beam. Constructed in GRP/foam sandwich, with 4-6 berths depending on layout.

Bradwell 18

This was moulded by Swin Mouldings, Lock Hill, Heybridge Basin, Maldon, Essex. They also built the Bradwell 22 Fishing Cruiser as shown.

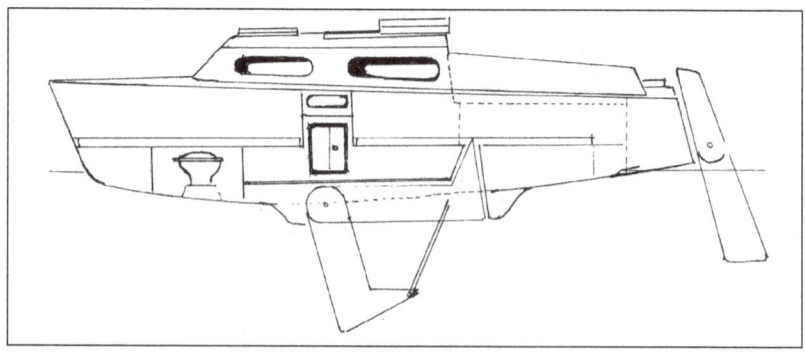

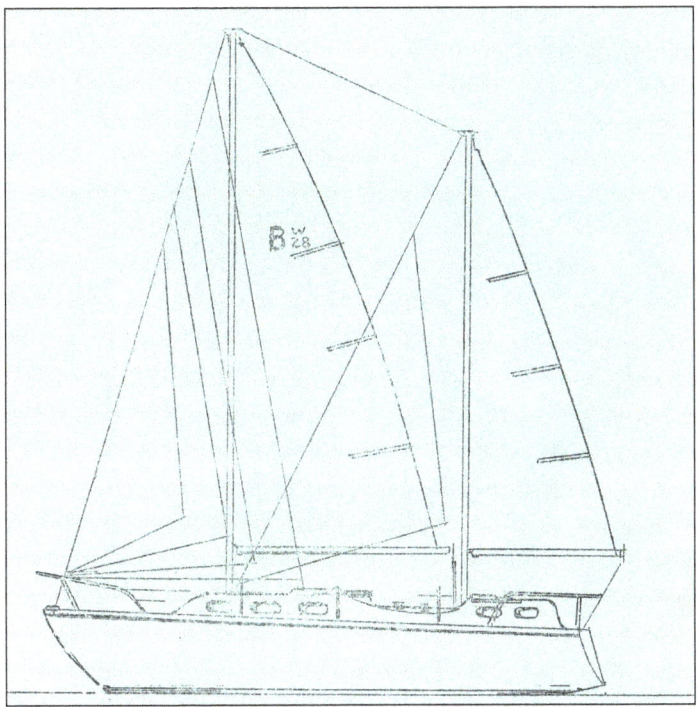

Bradwell 28 Centre Cockpit Ketch

Bradwell 22 Fishing Cruiser

Heybridge Basin

At the pub on the quayside I remember my father buying us ginger beer served from stone bottles.

The entrance to the canal, which runs all the way to Chelmsford, where horse drawn barges would carry their cargoes.

Heybridge Basin Lock and cottage

Originally established by act of Parliament and built between 1793-1797, the waterway has continued for over 200 years.

It went into neglect after the wood trade slowed up and the locks became derelict. During this period, in the late 1950s and early 1960s there was an annual canoe race, the course of which ran from Chelmsford to Heybridge basin, some eleven miles. I took part in the junior section of this race for some years, winning it on three occasions, once by a

Mike Davies winning the junior Chelmsford-Heybridge Canoe Race
Photo taken by Essex County Newspapers

'Scimitar' in Heybridge Basin

very close margin as seen in the photograph.

In later years I would sail my own yachts into the basin – always an enjoyable mooring for the night. The photograph shows my Cheverton Crusader in the Basin in 1986.

For many years they rented out moorings along the canal banks and their business was looked after by the canal lock keeper, in the 1960-1980s George Clark and later by the current lock keeper Colin Edmond.

The company running the canal changed and is now run by Essex Waterways Ltd, a division of Inland Waterways Association. The Chelmer Canal Trust was formed in 1995 to care for the canal.

Heybridge Basin and the canal are well used today with all the locks to Chelmsford having been renovated.

THE COMPANY OF THE PROPRIETORS OF THE
CHELMER & BLACKWATER NAVIGATION LTD.
Registered in England No. 130459   VAT Reg. No. 103 6589 76

SECRETARY & REGISTERED OFFICE:
PAPER MILL LOCK, LITTLE BADDOW, CHELMSFORD, ESSEX CM3 4BF
TELEPHONE: DANBURY 2025

Holt & James Yard

HOLT & JAMES

Set up by Arthur Holt and later joined by James MacMillan to becomes Holt & James. A number of boats were built here including the smack 'Ostrea Rose' (around 1980) for Michael Emmett, who worked her for a while then refitted her for charter.

The yard was taken over by Clint Swann in the early 2000s, the tea rooms refurbished and run by Wilkins & Co from Tiptree and yard buildings let out.

'Ostrea Rose'

Stebbens Boatyard, Heybridge Basin

STEBBENS BOATYARD

Along the sea wall downstream is Stebbens Boatyard. They built a number of yachts including the Holiwell Sloop, a clinker built 21.5' centreboard sloop as below.

Holiwell Sloop

Maldon Quay

Maldon

A mile or two upstream lies the town of Maldon, famous for Thames Barges which continue to use the town quay.

Walter Cook & Son

Walter Cook was born in Wivenhoe on December 20th 1862. The family moved to Brightlingsea when he was about four years old. At about 17 years old he was bound apprentice to Root & Diaper, boat builders in

Walter Cook's Yard in 2008

Brightlingsea – the yard later taken over by Douglas Stone from London.

At the end of his apprenticeship he moved to Maldon to work for John Howard who built barges in the yard now known as Dan Webb & Feesey. He moved to Nash & Miller at Battersea who built lighters.

In 1893 Walter moved back to Maldon and worked again at Howard's yard. In 1894 he set up business with Arthur Woodward in Finch's old yard, which was bought by James Keeble and leased to them, trading as Cook & Woodward. Part of this arrangement was that they built Keeble a barge on a cost-plus basis. In 1897 they built 'Dawn'.

In 1907-8 the partnership was dissolved and Walter continued as Walter Cook, Boat Builder.

Primarily building and repairing barges, from 1895-1905 they built Thames Barges 'Dawn', 'Lord Roberts' and 'British King' all three of which are in service today.

Also at this yard was built the prototype of the 27' Admiralty Montague Whaler and many more afterwards – other wooden craft for the Admiralty were also built through two world wars. Partly due to a fire and also because of lack of space, some boat building was carried out by Walter Cook at premises owned by Sadds and Maldon Salt Works.

In the 1960s the yard was in the hand of Barry Pearce and later Roger Beckett of Anglia Yacht Services Ltd.

A history of the yard was written by Clifford Cook and published by Joan M Cook sometime after Clifford Cook died in 1979.

Dan Webb & Feesey

Boat building has been going on in Maldon for many years and one of the well known yards is Dan Webb & Feesey.

Started by Dan Webb (who previously worked in the Colne Shipyards) in 1921 by re-opening the Shipways yard, he designed and built a number of yachts including in 1929 'Dodo' 33.2' twin screw with lug rig. In 1932 he built 'Undine' probably one of the first 18' Blackwater

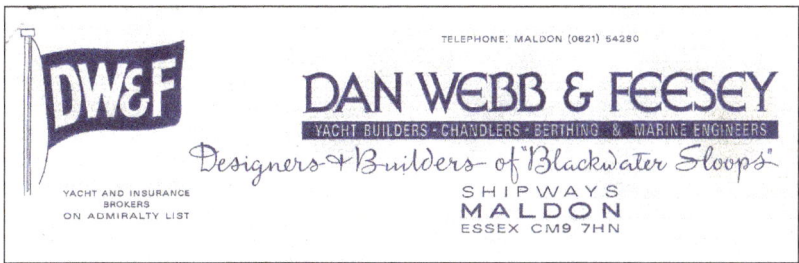

Dan Webb & Feesey

Sloops for which he was to become well known. These pretty craft were originally gaff rig and after the war were built with Bermudian rig and extended cabin sides, right forward to the stem. Most were long keel but some were built a centreboarders.

A 4 tonner at 22' was also built and Dan Webb was joined by Mr Feesey just after the war and they continued to build the Blackwater Sloop and later built three larger versions at 23' 6", 'Phylla' (below) being one I had placed on my brokerage list.

The letterhead below shows Meiklejohn & Wade Ltd who were running the yard in the 1960s and in late 1976 John Swinton, of Swinton and Wilkingson, took over the yard and copyrights to the Blackwater Sloops and ran it until he sold it in 1987. During this time the yard fitted out GRP hulls, the Blackwater 40 – see below (designed by John Bennett & Associates and moulded by Colvic as the Victor 40) and the Blackwater 48 (originally Trintella 48 designed by Van de Stadt) and carried on general refit and laying up work. They also took over Cardnells yard at Maylandsea (see chapter River Crouch).

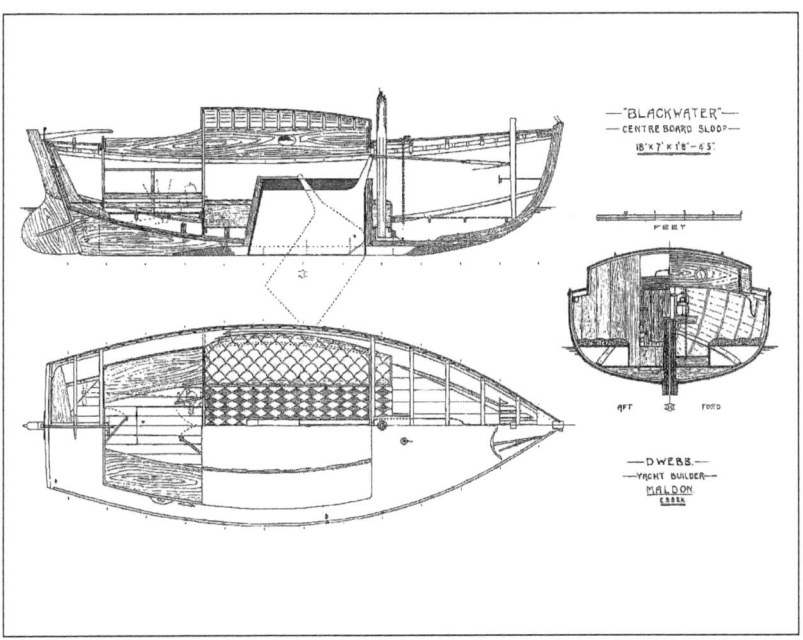

Blackwater Sloop

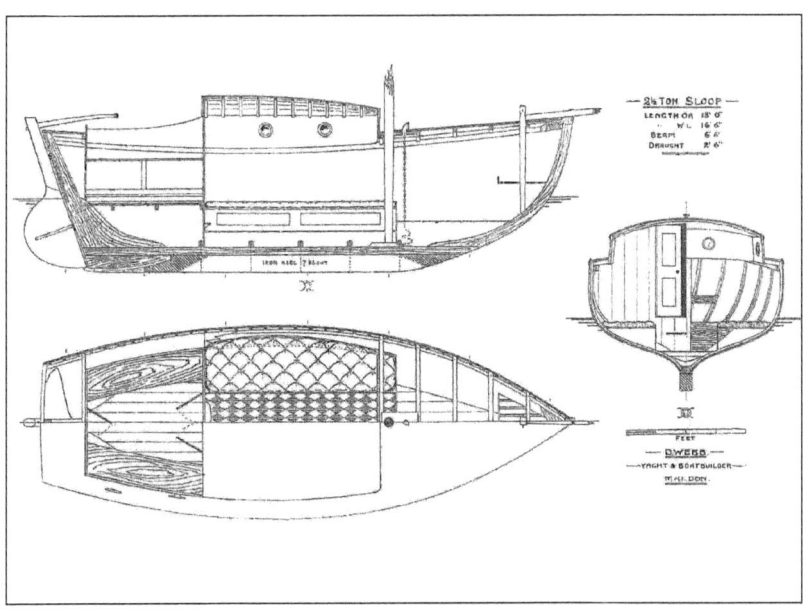

(Drawings supplied by John Swinton whilst running Dan Webb & Feesey)

Blackwater Sloop (earlier)

Blackwater Sloop (later) with full width coachroof taken forward

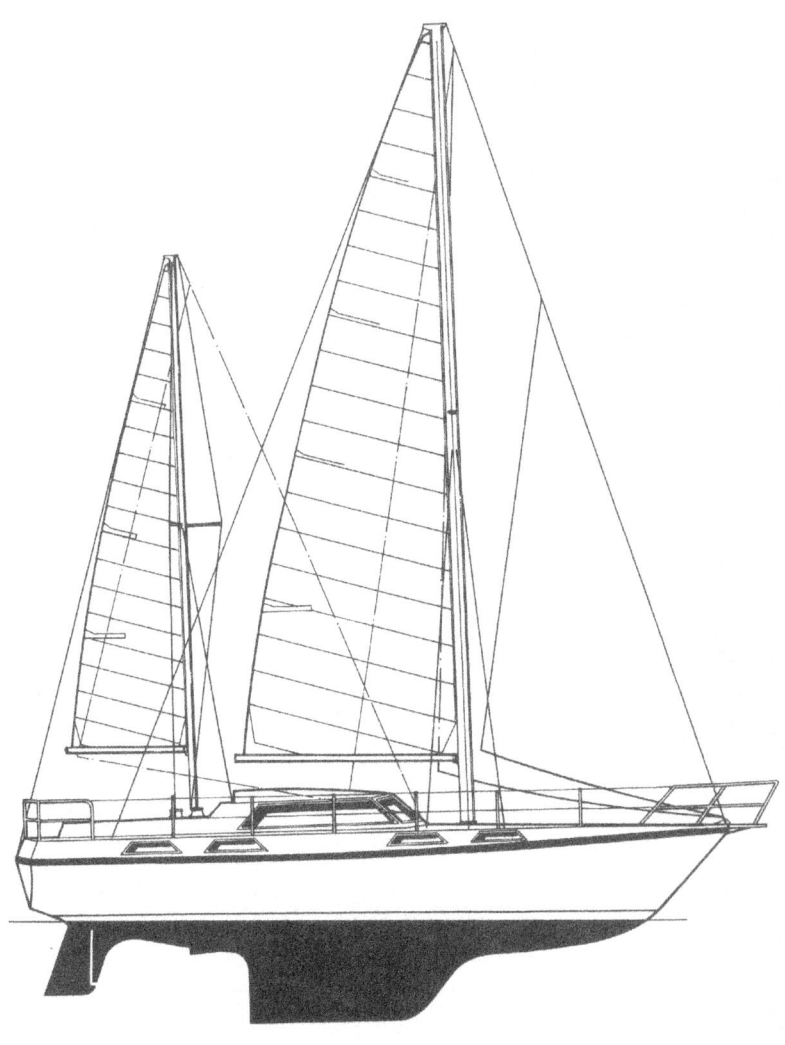

Blackwater 40

'Phylla' 23' 6"

HEDGECOCK & SON

Upstream and next to Dan Webb & Feesey was a small yard Hedgecock & Son, which was operating in the early 1900s – Walter Cook built them a boat named 'Favorite' around 1908 which carried passengers off the Maldon Hard. When I visited the yard from 1973 onwards it was run by Tom Hedgecock and his son Roger. They laid yachts up and provided engine repairs and also ran hire boats and day trippers further down past the quay in the summer months.

The yard was taken over in the 1990s by Noddy Cardy who carries on mud berthing and laying up and also dredging and piling.

DIXON KERLY

Still further upstream is an area known as 'The Downs'. In the 1930s the yard was owned by Charles Barker and Dixon Kerly developed it to build and repair yachts, it later being taken over by Mr C D Richardson and W J Tubbs. During their ownership in the 1960s they built a number of East Anglian Restricted Class 27.7' LOA designed by Alan Buchanan. Some of the hulls were built in Spain and completed at the yard.

Hedgecock & Son

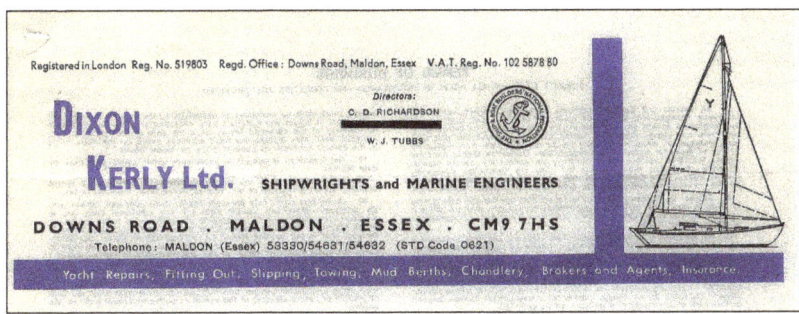

Miss Forrester ably looked after the office and dealt with the brokerage side of the business.

They also built another similar sloop, the Queen Bee class, designed by A.K.Balfour.

Long keel, carvel planked with raked transom 27' 9" LOA with a beam of 8' 6".

In 1979 the yard was put on the market and sold to a company named Caterelle Ltd comprising a syndicate of local people and has been trading since as Downs Road Boatyard.

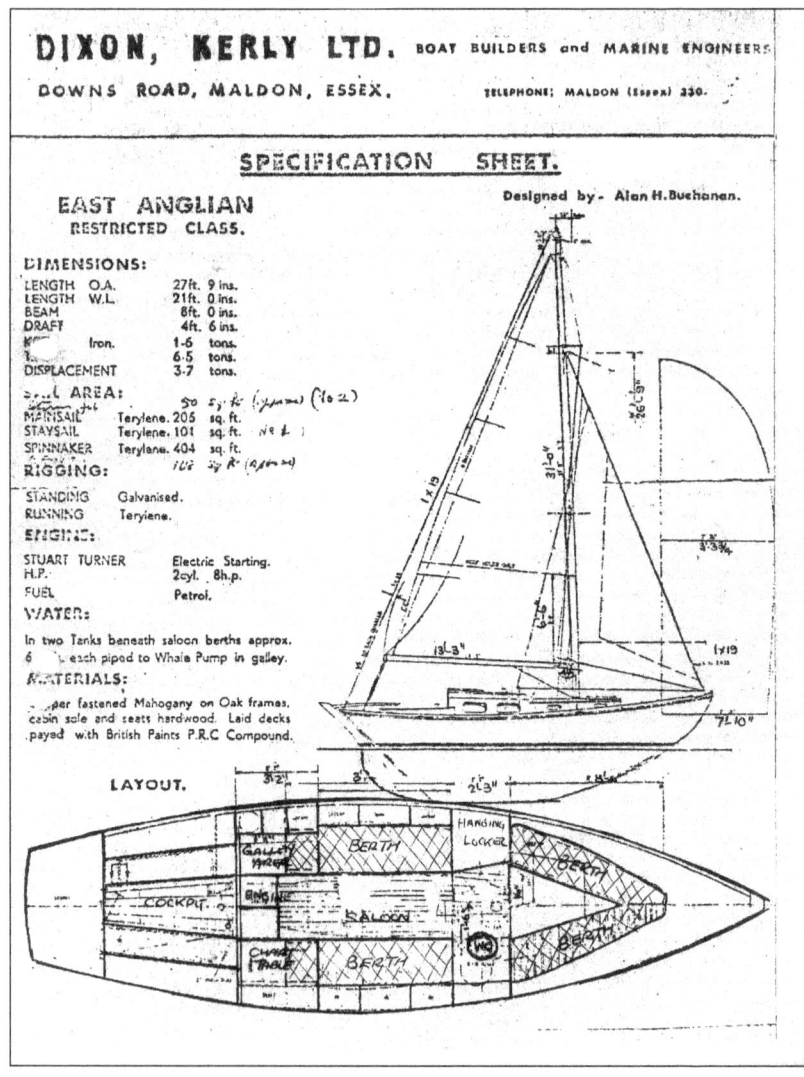

MIKE DAVIES

Dixon Kerly Boatyard

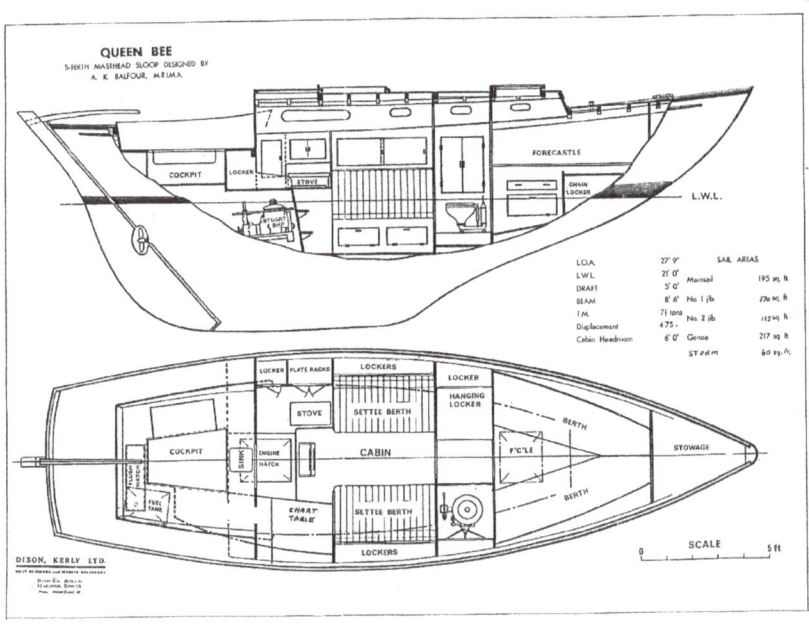

Queen Bee Sloop

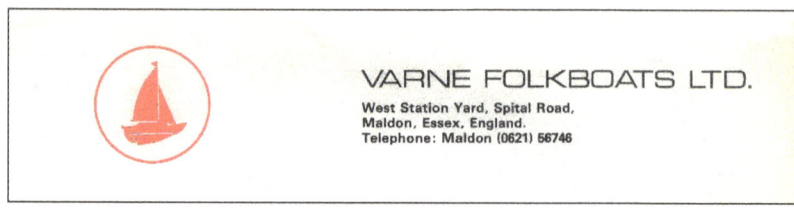

Varne Marine

Set up in 1973 by businessman Walter Standing, originally on Canvey Island, moving later to Maldon.

In the mid 1970s Alan Hill designed the British Folkboat to be built in glass fibre.

It was accepted by The Folkboat Association of Great Britain and built by Varne Folkboats Ltd., Maldon, Essex. It was built with dispensation from the Scandinavian Yacht Racing Union to allow carvel hulls, inboard engines, a doghouse/and or long coachroof and the use of glass fibre in place of timber.

Varne Marine Ltd also built the Varne 27 at Canvey Island – about 80 were built.

They then built the Varne 850 in Maldon in 1977. After about 20 were built the moulds were purchased by Weston Boats around 1980, who marketed her as the Weston 850.

GRP British Folkboat

MIKE DAVIES

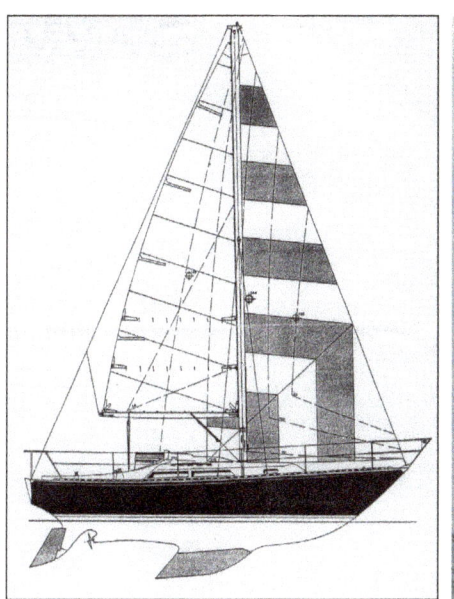

Varne 27   Varne 850

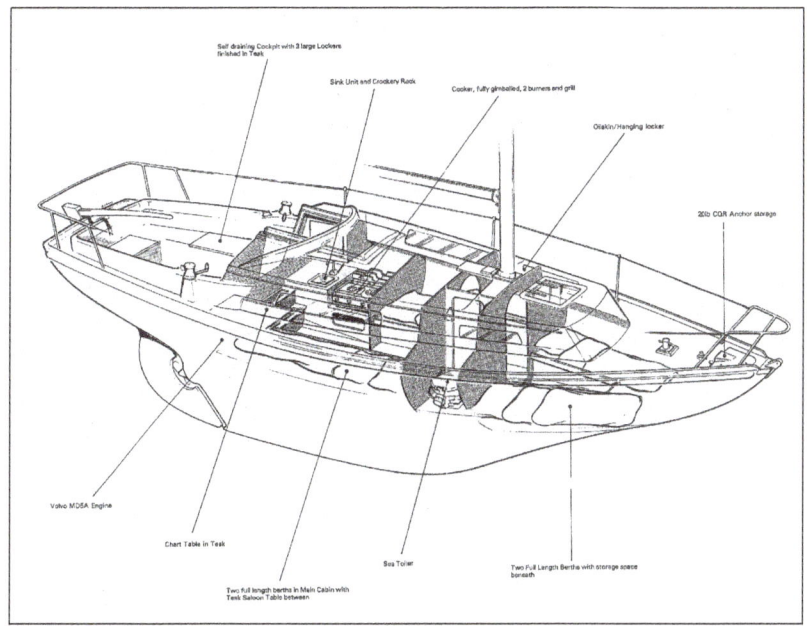

CHAPTER 8

THE RIVERS CROUCH AND ROACH

THE RIVER CROUCH LIES SOUTH of the Blackwater and runs almost due west inland for several miles, with the River Roach branching off after about four miles and running south.

River Roach

An interesting story about the Roach concerns Charles Darwin's, 'Beagle' in which he made his famous voyages. She ended her days as a watch vessel to combat smuggling in the Southend Coastguard District

On a chart produced in 1847 by the Photographic Office Survey Team it shows the Beagle moored in the middle of the River Roach. In 1850 the ship was moved ashore to a spot, which the coastguard controller and his officers considered she should be berthed. A recent archaeological survey found much mid-Victorian pottery that came from the ship. Further investigation revealed the shape and size of a dock with something on the bottom, believed to be a ship. The investigation continues.

The river Roach runs off due south for a mile or so and then bends westwards and splits into two creeks, Paglesham Reach being the main part and off to port Yokesfleet Creek.

On both these creeks lie boatyards.

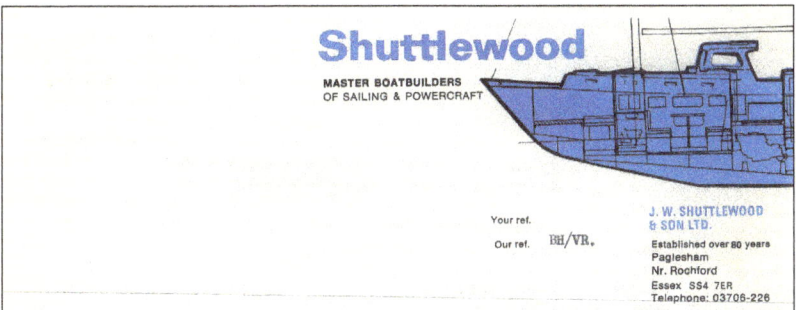

SHUTTLEWOODS

Shuttlewoods yard is on the west bank of Paglesham Creek just through Paglesham Eastend village. In 1848, the predecessor of James Shuttlewood, William Kemp, is recorded as having built the oyster smack 'Kate' at Paglesham. James Shuttlewood continued to build Thames barges around 1890 and one, 'Ethel Ada', is still afloat. Frank Shuttlewood succeeded his father in the 1930s and continued to build boats for the

Shuttlewoods Boatyard 2008

River front at Shuttlewoods Boatyard 2008

growing pleasure market, formerly called F W Shuttlewood & Sons and changed to J W Shuttlewood & Sons around the late 1950s.

F W Shuttlewood & Sons built many wooden yachts during the 1930s, 1940s and 1950s, many rigged as gaff cutters and designed by F W Shuttlewood.

Old boat building sheds on river front at Shuttlewoods Boatyard 2008

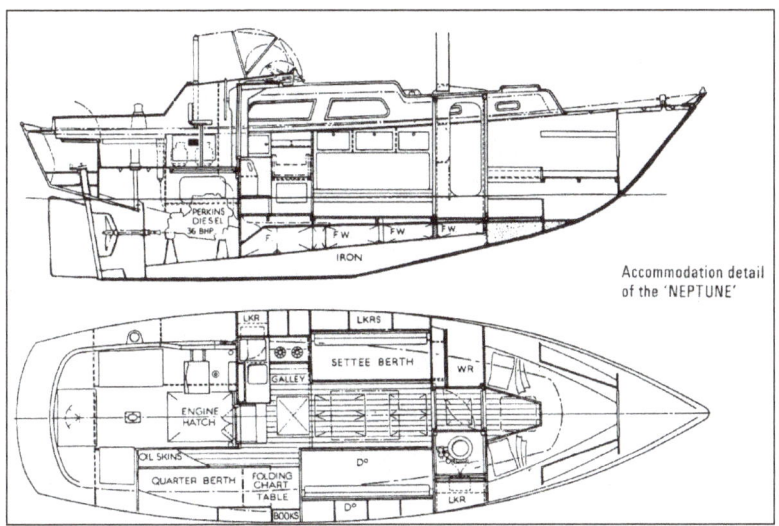

Accommodation detail of the 'NEPTUNE'

Neptune

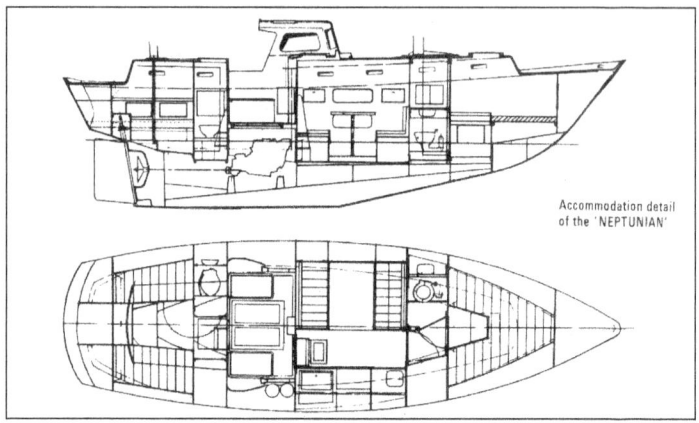

Neptunian

In 1932 'Secret', a 28' gaff cutter was built, 1936 'Dione', 30.5' gaff cutter, 1937 'Bird of Dawning' 30' gaff cutter (still sailing today), 1947 Jennie 25' gaff cutter, 1951 'Levanter' 36' cutter, 1958 'Kulu' 40.9' ketch, 1956 'Tiny Mite' a 35.2'spritsail barge – all designed by F W Shuttlewood.

Wooden yachts continued to be built in the 1960s with 'La Cucuracha' 26.6' c/board sloop designed by F Shuttlewood in 1962 and in 1964 'Lady Camelot' 32.5' sloop designed by Alan Buchanan.

With the advent of glass fibre in the late 1950s and early 1960s, the yard started to fit out two motor sailers designed by Alan Buchanan, the Neptune (sloop rig) and Neptunian (ketch rig), both using the same 32.75' long keel hull. They built many of these, all to Lloyds +100A1. See drawings below.

Essex Yacht Builders Limited
Wallasea Island, Nr, Rochford, Essex, England
Telephone Canewdon 531/5 (STD) 03-706 531/5

Essex Yacht Builders Limited reserve the right to change specifications and prices without notice.

In 1987 the yard was taken over by David Barke (previously of the Quay Maldon) and his sons who continue to lay up yachts, offer engineering work and sell new power craft.

They traded under Essex Boatyards Ltd and recently reverted back to the original name Shuttlewoods Boatyard.

WALLASEA ISLAND

A few miles up the road and north to the River Crouch lies Wallasea Island where there has been a marina for many years.

I visited them on several occasions during the 1970s and 1980s when it was in the hands of Tartan Arrow Marine.

During this time Essex Yacht Builders Ltd was building the Cleopatra range of fast power craft from 700 series, 850 series and 1000 series – see two models pictured below.

They also built the Salar 40, a centre cockpit sloop designed by Laurent Giles & Partners, measuring 39' 6" x 11' 0" x 5' 3".

Cleopatra 700 Sports Fisherman

Cleopatra 850 Family Cruiser

With Compliments

Boat Sales and Administration
Telephone: (01702) 258885 Fax: 258441
E-mail: sales@essexboatyards.com
web: www.essexboatyards.com

Essex Boatyards Ltd, Essex Marina
Wallasea Island, Essex. SS4 2HF
(01702) 258885

Marina & Harbour Master
Telephone: (01702) 258531 Fax: 258227
E-mail: info@essexmarina.co.uk
web: www.essexmarina.co.uk

Essex Marina 2008

MIKE DAVIES

Essex Marina bar/restaurant, offices and yard 2008

In 2005 David Barke took over the marina under the trading name of Essex Boatyards Ltd with the marina trading as Essex Marina.

There has been much work carried out to update the marina and boatyard and they are agents for several power craft including Fairline.

SUTTONS BOATYARD

Tucked in behind Potton Island at Gt Wakering is Suttons Boatyard, where boat builder E W Sutton built many wooden yachts in the 1950s and 1960s to designs by Guy Thompson, Alan Buchanan and Robert Clark. The yard became Sutton & Wiggins Ltd and around 1970 Sutton & Smith and carried on building wooden yachts,

'Surian Too' in 1970, 32.5' to Alan Buchanan design, 'Thirza' in 1972, 27.9'.

Sometime in the late 1970s the yard was taken over by Ivan Furness and his wife.

They also traded as Chandler & Smith and in 1959 they designed

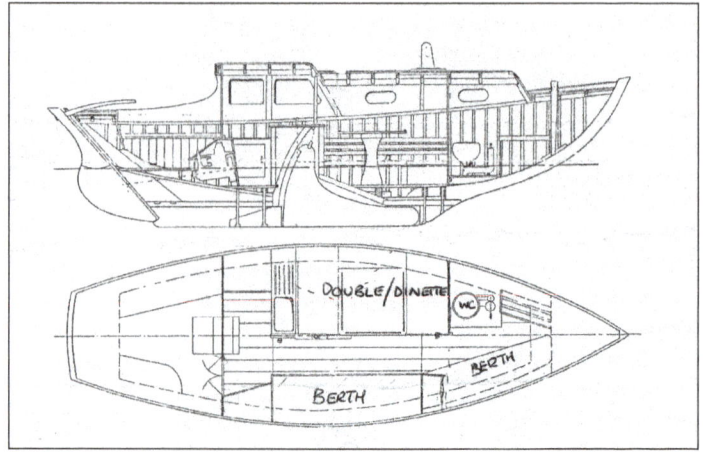

Mapleleaf Centreboard Sloop

and built a delightful centreboard sloop called the Mapleleaf, being 22' 9" LOA with a beam of 7' 6", clinker built mahogany on Canadian Rock Elm.

In 1968 they built the first of a larger sister yacht, the Oakleaf, being 27' 6" LOA and a beam of 8' 3", also with a centreboard. Clinker built of African mahogany on Rock Elm frames. The photograph below was supplied to me by her owner in 1983 and the one ashore I took in 1984.

Oakleaf Sloop No 1 'Engelska'

Hunter Boats

Another prolific builder of yachts not actually with sea front premises is Hunter Boats, who started life near the marshes at Wakering close to Rochford.

In 1968 the company was called Essex Boat Company and first moulded the National Squib designed by Oliver Lee and finished off by him. They are still built today but not by Hunter Boats. Some 800 or more have been built. With its tanned sails they are easily recognised.

A year or two later Peter Poland (of Hunter Boats) asked Oliver Lee to design a lid for the Squib to enable cross Channel JOG racing and hence the Hunter 19 was conceived. The Hunter Europa quickly followed with larger cabin and generally more comfortable throughout.

Oliver Lee designed all the early Hunter boats including the 16' Hunter 490 with lifting keel, the 23' Hunter 701, the Tracer (smaller Squib with lifting keel).

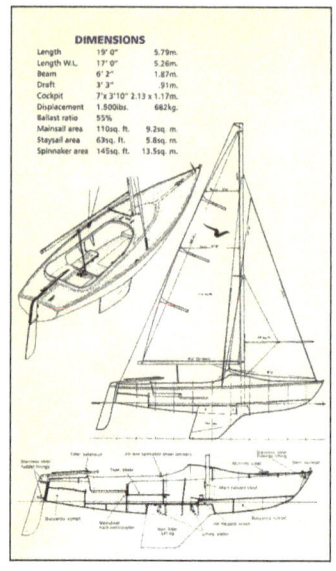 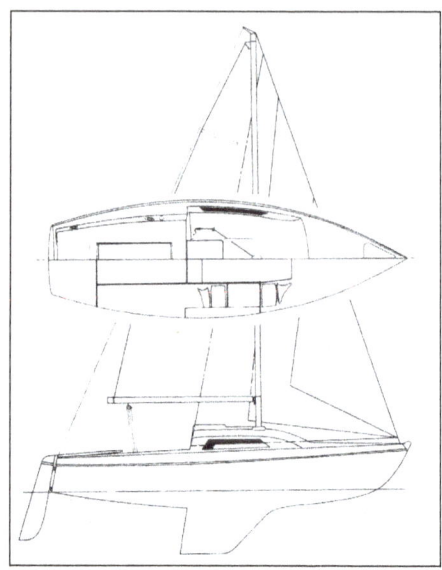

National Squib   Hunter Europa Mk II

Designer David Thomas then produced many later Hunters, the Sonata in 1975 which gained RYA National Status as a class.

In 1977 the Impala 28 appeared as an Offshore One Design cruiser or racer.

Hunter Sonata

Hunter Impala 28 OOD

Hunter Minstrel 23

There followed the Hunter Delta 25, lifting keel Medina 20 and the more unorthodox cat rigged ketch centreboarder the Hunter Liberty. Her sister was the gaff rigged Minstrel 23.

Hunter Delta 25

Hunter Horizon 26

Hunter Horizon 32

Hunter Channel 32

The Hunter Delta 25, a lifting keel trailerable cruiser appeared around 1980. In 1984 a very popular model was introduced – the Hunter Horizon 26 with bilge keels or fin keel – she won Best Production Boat of the Year Award.

The Hunter 27, 272 and 273 followed and the Hunter 32 Wheelhouse Cruiser. This won Award for the best Production Cruiser in 1987.

The last Horizon models built were the 21, 23, and 30, mostly with bilge keels.

In 1991 the Hunter Channel 32 was built, being the largest in the range, in bilge keels and fin keel.

1994 saw the introduction of the new Ranger hull shape, again

Hunter Ranger 265

designed by David Thomas, with longer waterlines giving more stability.

The Ranger 265 and 245 followed with the Pilot 27 with large deck saloon.

The Hunter 707 appeared in 1995 as a fast planning sports boat and gained the Yacht of the Year Award in 1996 having become one of the fastest keelboat classes.

In 1998 Hunter departed into a new realm by producing the Landau Cruiser for the Landau Launch Company and won the 1998 motorboat design competition, appearing first at the 1999 Boat Show. Two further models have been added, the Landau 20 Walkabout and Landau 29 Continental. It is worth noting that Hunters had produced a power boat before, way back in the early years – this was the Hunter Jetcruiser 20, a re-designed version of the Hamilton Jet 20, originally from New Zealand.

The Channel 31 was launched in 2000 and in 2003 the Mystery 35 appeared.

In 2003 Hunter Boats was taken over by the Select Yacht Group which also has Cornish Crabbers, Red Fox Yachts, the Landau Launch Company and Cornish Diva.

The business continues today.

The River Crouch

Burnham-on-Crouch is the first town to appear on the north bank and has been a centre of boat building and yachting for well over a century.

Sometimes referred to as the Cowes of the East Coast, well known classes race there today including Dragons and Stellas, where many of these classes have been built over the years.

ESSEX AND SUFFOLK BOATYARDS AND BOAT BUILDERS

THE ALBATROSS CLASS

A 20 Ton Steel Motor Sailer

Designed by Alan H. Buchanan

LOA 42'   LWL 32'   Beam 11' 10"
Draft 5' 6"   Displacement 13.31 Tons

A YACHT DESIGNED FOR WORLD-WIDE CRUISING, she is Ketch rigged with a working sail area of 777 sq. ft. and powered by a B.M.C. Commodore Diesel.

Her construction is all welded steel which has been specially treated to resist rust and corrosion. Decks are of Teak laid on ply with P.R.C. rubberised caulking. The superstructure is all of Teak, also the cockpit and coamings. Masts and spars are Silver Spruce. All work is of the finest finish.

The accommodation is well designed with berths for five or six persons. Galley and toilet are lined with Formica and have tiled floors.

Water Tank capacity is 90 gals. Fuel tanks 180 gals.

The price of the standard yacht is £9000 subject to any fluctuation in the cost and availability of the steel hulls.

STEBBINGS (BURNHAM) LTD

CHAPEL ROAD . BURNHAM-ON-CROUCH . ESSEX

TELEPHONE 2126

Printed by The Crouch Press, 114 Station Road, Burnham-on-Crouch, Essex

The Royal Corinthian Yacht Club

Much has changed over the years with many of the old boat yards disappearing under housing schemes. Yardleys, J King, Burnham Yacht Building Company and Stebbings are a few now long gone.

Stebbings built a number of yachts including this one, The Albatross Class, designed by Alan Buchanan and built in welded steel with teak decks and superstructure.

Royal Burnham Yacht Club

RICE & COLE LTD.
RIVER MOORINGS . YACHT REPAIRS . OSMOSIS AND RESPRAY CENTRE
YACHT BROKERS AND CHANDLERS . COUNTRY CARAVAN PARK PROPRIETORS

SEA END BOATHOUSE
BURNHAM-ON-CROUCH
ESSEX CM0 8AN
TELEPHONE : 01621 782063
FAX : 01621 786741

E-MAIL : ricoltd@aol.com
YACHT SALES : 01621 784211
CARAVAN SALES : 01621 784211

The river frontage all alone the river bank has been cleaned up and an attractive walkway now runs from the sea end before the Royal Corinthian Yacht Club up beyond what was one of Tucker Brown boatyards, past private houses, yacht clubs, restaurants and boatyards.

RICE & COLE
The first boatyard coming up the river is Rice & Cole.
The yard was started in 1935 by Tom Rice (who had been foreman at

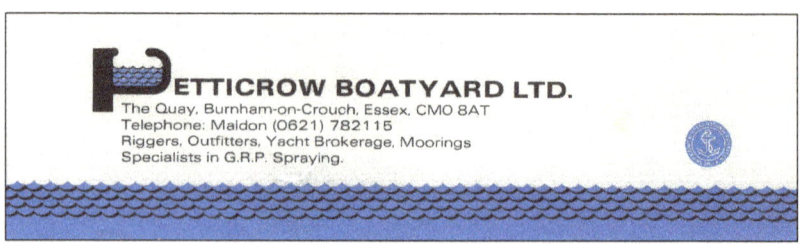

PETTICROW BOATYARD LTD.
The Quay, Burnham-on-Crouch, Essex, CM0 8AT
Telephone: Maldon (0621) 782115
Riggers, Outfitters, Yacht Brokerage, Moorings
Specialists in G.R.P. Spraying.

The Quay, Burnham-on-Crouch, Essex, CM0 8AT
Tel: +44 (0)1621 782115 Fax: +44 (0)1621 785389
One Design Racing Yachts
Email: Petticrows@Petticrows.com
Web site: http://www.Petticrows.com

Petticrow's new premises

Petticrows) and Bill Cole. In about 1938 at the beginning of WWII they moved to the Maltings (near Priors) and carried out various work including net making for the war effort.

At the end of the war they moved back to Sea End Boathouse and carried on their refit and laying up work to this present day. The yard never actually built new boats.

Around 1963 Tom Rice left to take over the Victory Pub in Providence, Burnham-on-Crouch and Mr Anderson joined the firm.

The present directors are Nick Oliver and J Lyon-Hall and H Oliver.

PETTICROWS LTD

Next door to Rice & Cole are the new premises of Petticrows Ltd who had previously been trading as Newell Petticrow from around 1900 in buildings behind the Corinthian Yacht Club. These having been demolished some

Original site of William King & Sons – now housing. The red sheds are part of R J Prior & Son

years ago and replaced with Petticrow Quays, a housing development.

Petticrows has built a variety of yachts including Stella and Dragons and now produce the all glass fibre Dragon, the plug of which was constructed by John Mullins.

Just up from the Royal Burnham Yacht Club is another new housing development, which used to be the location of William King and Sons.

WILLIAM KING & SON

William King & Son was started around 1900 by William King who came from Wivenhoe. He started repairing and building yachts. In 1907 he built 'Lona III' a 35.5' sloop designed by J Pain Clark. Over the years he built several designs by J Pain Clark and also the East Coast One Designs designed by G U Laws. 'Chittabob', 'Delphine' and 'Widgeon' to name some of them – all 30' racing yachts, originally gaff rig. They also built the Royal Burnham One Design.

Herbert Page had joined the firm in 1922 as an apprentice.

In 1924 Morgan King became a partner.

The yard later built 'Lisbet' a 24.5' Norman Dallimore design in 1938.

During the WWII years the yard built a number of Motor Torpedo Boats and an MFV.

From about 1946, Herbert Page (he was married to Alice King) ran the yard with Stan King, employing about 30 people.

After the war yacht building started again and in 1947 built 'Kirmew' 24.7' designed by Robert Clark.

In 1952 'Wanderer III' was built for Eric Hiscock in which he completed his circumnavigation of the world (designed by Laurent Giles & Partners).

'Yuletide', 27.7' was built in 1965 to a design by Alan Buchanan.

These are just a few of the yachts William King & Son built over the years – Lloyds Register of Yachts lists many more.

In 1975 the yard ceased trading and later the site was cleared and new homes built on it (see photograph above).

R J Prior & Son

R. J. PRIOR & SON (BURNHAM) LTD.,
QUAYSIDE,
BURNHAM-ON-CROUCH,
ESSEX.
CM0 8AS.
Telephone: 0621 782160

Near the old site of William King & Son is R J Prior & Son, which was started in 1892 by Frederick Prior and known as F J Prior & Sons, repairing Thames barges and fishing boats. They bought land at Buckingham Square in 1892.

The first boat built was 'Altair' in 1909.

In 1915 they purchased the wharf. In 1933 Fred Prior died and Reg Prior took over and constructed the buildings on the wharf – naming the yard R J Prior & Son, as it is known today and continued to build yachts.

In 1937 they built the 'Vanguard' an oyster dredger for the Smith Brothers.

World War II came and like many other boatyards, Priors built a number of pinnaces and whalers.

In 1940, on 1st January, Murray Prior joined the firm (now deceased)

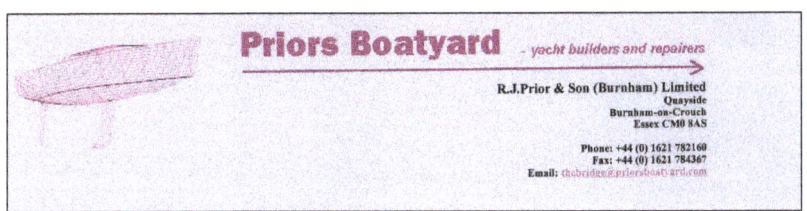

R J Prior & Son

and is still active in it today with his son Robin who joined in the 1980s and continues to run the yard.

They built many yachts including some designed by Alan Buchanan.

I owned 'Timba' a Prior 30 built in 1967 and one of a dozen of the class built to a Chris Petrie design. Later in the glass fibre era, Priors built the Prior Passage Maker, a capable motorsailer.

PRIOR "30"

LENGTH	30 ft. 0 in.
LWL	22 ft. 6 in.
BEAM	9 ft. 0 in.
DRAFT	5 ft. 0 in.
SAIL AREA (RORC)	392 sq. ft.
BALLAST RATIO	48%
RORC RATING	17.15
DESIGNER	C. PETRIE

R. J. PRIOR & SON
(BURNHAM) LTD.

BURNHAM-ON-CROUCH . ESSEX
TELEPHONE BURNHAM-ON-CROUCH 2190

MIKE DAVIES

| TELEPHONE **2150** | **Tucker Brown & Co.** Limited BURNHAM-ON-CROUCH ESSEX |

TUCKER BROWN

Tucker Brown was founded in 1906 by Andrew Bigmore, Joe Cole and R J S (Stan) Tucker buying land adjoining the sea wall and supplied moorings and fitted out yachts.

After World War 1 Stan Tucker left the firm to found Crouch Engineering, which remains in the family today, being run by Stan's grand-

Tucker Brown old premises, Coronation Road

175

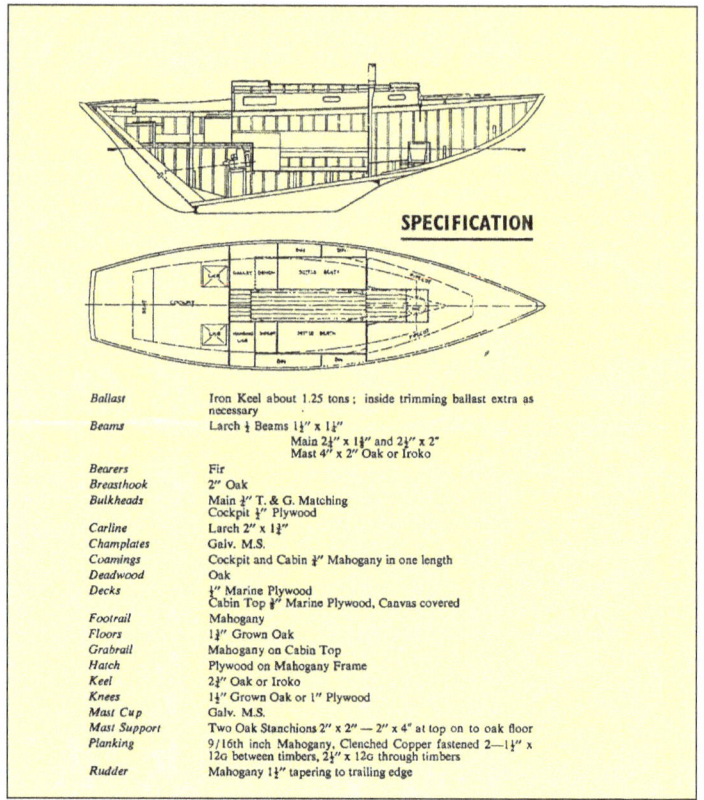

Stella Class

son Jonathon Tucker.

Tucker Brown took over J King, a nearby boat builder and began to build and design yachts.

The business continued to expand and had premises in Coronation Road which are still there.

World War II came and with it a change at the yard when Sonny and Bob Cole took over after the original partners retired.

In 1947 they built 'Blue Bonnet' a 39' ketch to Norman Dalimore design.

'Elusive Lady' was built in 1953 to Guy Thompson design and in 1956 'Sabrina Fair' to a C E Nicholson design.

Tucker Brown also built a large number of the Stella Class clinker sloops designed by Holman & Pye – some one hundred and ten were built but several were built at other yards. The Stella still races as a class at Burnham Week and has an active Class Association.

Changes were coming to boat building with the advent of glass fibre in the late 1950s and in 1967 Tucker Brown fitted out 'Zorina' a 35.3'grp hull moulded by Thames Marine Ltd and designed by Holman & Pye. They fitted out several more GRP hulls and built many more wooden yachts through the 1960s and 1970s to designs by Holman & Pye, Alan Hill, A P Gurney, Guy Thompson and others.

For a brief period around 1980 Mike Hemingway and Ken Smith owned the business but sold it and the yard was closed. A museum is now housed in the Coronation Road buildings – see photo above.

Burnham Marina

On the extreme up-river end of Burnham-on-Crouch is located the Burnham Marina, originally developed by Mike Hemingway after he sold Tucker Browns in 1989. Planning permission was in place around 1987 and this drawing shows the proposed layout at the time.

In 2003 the marina was sold to Shotley Marina Holdings Ltd who have continued to expand and improve the facilities.

With over 350 berths, a 35 ton travel hoist and 100 ton slip, the marina can handle large craft and have an extensive workshop to compliment their facilities. A large chandlery was opened in 2004 and Clarke & Carter Interyacht Ltd run one of their offices here.

The Swallowtail restaurant has a large selection of food available.

Burnham Marina

ESSEX AND SUFFOLK BOATYARDS AND BOAT BUILDERS

Burnham Yacht Harbour Marina Limited

WITH COMPLIMENTS

BURNHAM YACHT HARBOUR BURNHAM-ON-CROUCH ESSEX CM0 8BL
TEL: 01621 782150 FAX: 01621 785848 E-MAIL: admin@burnhamyachtharbour.co.uk

BURNHAM-ON-CROUCH YACHT HARBOUR

Proposed layout drawing

Burnham Marina

FERRO CEMENT MARINE SERVICES

Not a new material to the marine world, concrete commercial vessels had been built as far back as the early 1900s, in Italy and also later here. Two concrete motorised sailing cargo vessels were built, one of them 'Moliette' ended up as a gunnery target off East Mersea (see chapter 1).

The ferro cement period of yacht building took off in the 1960s and lasted about twenty years. Sadly, years later, one came across part built hulls in boat yards and gardens where dreams had failed to materialise.

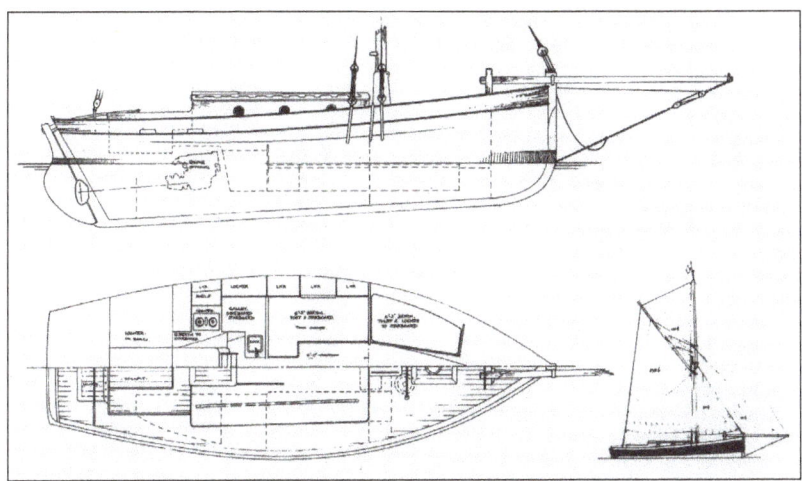

32' 8" Bawley designed by Alan Hill

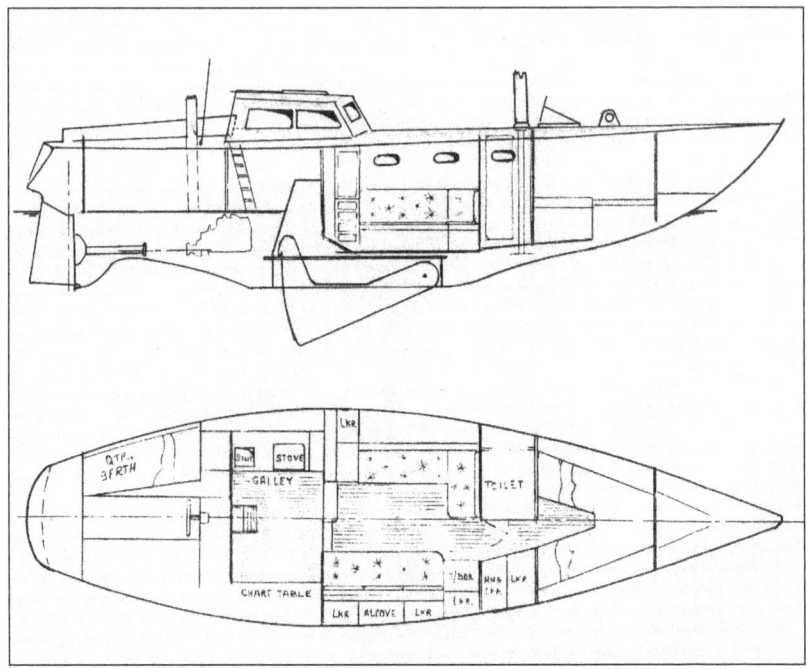

Above: 40' Centre Board Ketch designed by Alan Hill •Below: 38' Ketch

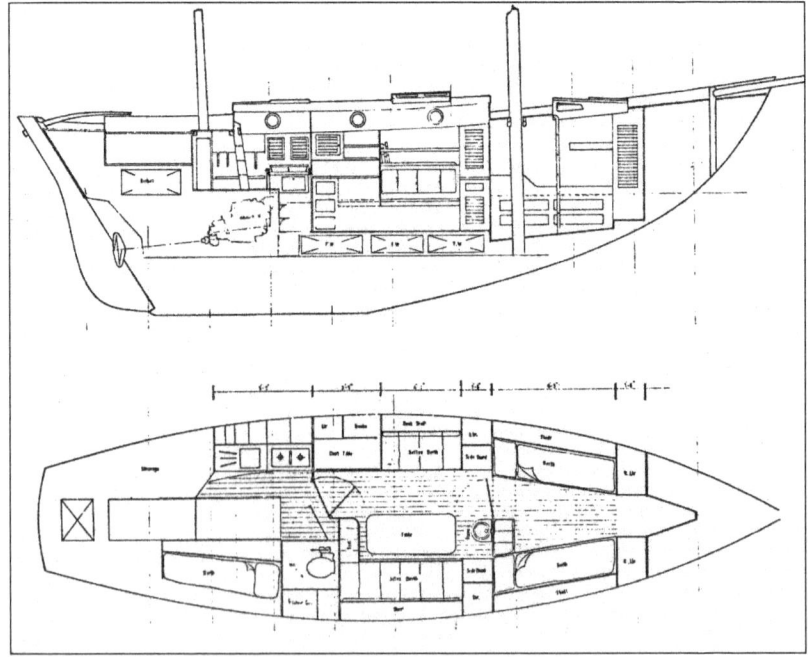

FERRO CEMENT MARINE SERVICES

160 Station Road, Burnham-on-Crouch, Essex.   Tel: Maldon (0621) 782971

One company involved in this market was set up by John Hodsdon and successfully traded a number of years, using the design skills of Alan Hill, John French and Chris Petrie to offer a fair number of designs to the public.

One advantage of ferro cement was that any shape could be produced without expensive moulds or jigs and the range of yachts on offer from John Hodsdon included smacks, bawleys, sloops, ketches, centreboard ketches and more. Some are shown here.

Continuing up river a few miles, the village of North Fambridge lies on the north bank.

NORTH FAMBRIDGE YACHT STATION

For many years since around the turn of the century a boatyard has existed behind the seawall, known as North Fambridge Yacht Station.

In the early 1970s Richard Stickney was running the yard that repaired, fitted out and laid up yachts. The manager then was Thornton Jones and Peter Pearson looked after the general running of the yard as manager from 1976 to 2003. He spent a number of years earlier working for R J Prior & Sons, Burnham-on-Crouch and is compiling a book on the history of the Burnham boatyards. In 1980 Ken Garget and Peter Hill took over North Fambridge Yacht Station. Ken Garget also was running West Wick Marina, a short way up the river.

Around the end of the 1990s the name changed slightly to North Fambridge Yacht Centre Ltd.

In April 2004 the Yacht Haven Group purchased both North Fambridge Yacht Station and West Wick Marina and now trades under the name Fambridge Yacht Haven.

There are 180 berths at the Yacht Haven and an 18 ton Travel Lift. At the Yacht Station there is a launch & recovery (dry sailing) facility, visitor's pontoons, mud berths and swinging and valet moorings.

NORTH FAMBRIDGE YACHT STATION LIMITED
NORTH FAMBRIDGE
Nr. CHELMSFORD
ESSEX CM3 6LR
Tel. Maldon (0621) 740370

Fambridge Yacht Station (originally North Fambridge Yacht Station)

Fambridge Yacht Haven (formerly West Wick Marina)

Fambridge Yacht Haven Ltd
Church Road
North Fambridge
Chelmsford
Essex CM3 6LR
Tel: (01621) 740370
Fax: (01621) 742359
Email: fambridge@yachthavens.com
Website: www.yachthavens.com

CHAPTER 9
LEIGH-ON-SEA AND CANVEY ISLAND

B OATYARDS AND BOAT BUILDERS ARE usually found on the seafront but one boat builder, Alan Platt, is hidden away in Thundersley, surrounded by trees in a delightful woodland setting, a few

Earlier letterhead

ESSEX AND SUFFOLK BOATYARDS AND BOAT BUILDERS

Later letterhead

miles north of Leigh-on-Sea.

I first met Alan Platt in 1981 when he was well into his boat building career and in November 2007 I called on him again to update information for this book.

Alan served his apprenticeship at Seacraft in Leigh-on-Sea from 1950-1956. In 1957 he was called up and went into the Royal Engineers, serving on tugs as a marine engineer. After this compulsory two years he set up on his own in 1959, buying an area of wooded land at Thundersley. He erected a temporary building shed and a house and one of the first boats he built was a plywood Heron sailing dinghy. He carried out alteration work on boats around Leigh-on-Sea area and in 1961 built an Alan Buchanan designed 25' long keel yacht, then two Maurice Griffiths Storm Class 26' carvel yachts. Around this time he met Laurie Harbotell who designed a 21' centre boarder for himself and asked Alan to build it. Alan's wife Shirley came up with the name Finesse and thus the beginning of a long run of yachts began.

Alan built around eighty of the 21' Finesses, the last being built around 1990.

The Finesse 24 was designed by Alan himself and again built around 80 of them up to around 1996. By this time Alan had perfected the technique for building these clinker yachts and despite voices of doubt, he made up sets of templates for all planking, which resulted in a faster building time. Of course during fitting, planks had to be shaped to fit but he reckoned he was building two Finesse 24s at a time, taking about 12 weeks to complete them. He also used a compressed air riveter, which speeded up the clenching of the copper nails and roves attaching the hull planking. Another innovation was the use of a spray gun to apply the undercoats to the newly planked hulls. This needed a little trial and

Original boat shed/machine shop

error before it was reasonably safe but in these days of 'health & safety' it wouldn't have got off the ground.

In 1983, in conjunction with Maurice Griffiths he built the Finesse 27 (or Finesse 28 as it is sometimes called) – a development of Maurice Griffiths 26' Bawley Class.

A number of these were built up to 1995.

Alan is retired now and has rebuilt the original boat shed as a fine wooden clad house (see photo).

Current home from original boatshed

ESSEX AND SUFFOLK BOATYARDS AND BOAT BUILDERS

Above: Finesse 21, Finesse 24 • Below: Finesse 27

Febris Marine

Located at Hockley, just south of the River Crouch, Febris Marine produced the 17' Lysander in glass fibre, in 1970s, designed by Percy Blandford and originally built in plywood. It is not known for how long or how many were built here.

FEBRIS MARINE
Hockley 6826.
32 HIGHAMS ROAD
HOCKLEY, ESSEX.

Lysander

Leigh-on-Sea

The waterfront at Leigh-on-Sea has for many years been a busy place for fishing boats trawling for fish, cockles, whelks and more and also boat builders, two of whom, Thomas Bundock and James Wiseman were in business in 1848.

Of the more current boatyards, some are detailed below.

L H Walker

A well known builder of clinker dinghies was L H Walker in Leigh-on-Sea who built his first Tideway in 1954. This was a 12' clinker built mahogany planked sailing dinghy, gunter rigged.

He built a range of dinghies from 8' to 14' and continued building up to 1979 when trading ceased and the frames were destroyed. Around 504 of the 12' dinghies were built and recorded as Tideways. Since 1980 other boat builders have produced the Tideway.

Seacraft

Seacraft were located at 8 High Street, Leigh-on-Sea and had been building boats from before the war. In 1948 they built the fishing boat 'Renown' and after the war a number of designs by Maurice Griffiths and Reg Freeman. The last yacht built is believed to be 'Sula', a Barcarole Class designed by Maurice Griffiths and the yard ceased trading in 1957. Alan Platt served his time here in the 1950s and went on the establish Finesse Yachts in 1959.

Sea King (Boatbuilders) Ltd

Sea King (Boatbuilders) Ltd was established by Reg Patten on 29th October 1958.

He had served his time at Dauntless pre-war and rose to become foreman before leaving and setting up Sea-King.

He built clinker planked yachts from 23 feet to 31 feet. Most had lifting keels enabling them to take the ground around their natural habitat on the East Coast.

SEA-KING (Boatbuilders) LTD.
8a, HIGH STREET, LEIGH-ON-SEA, ESSEX.

He built some 44 yachts, from 1959 to March 1967, thirty of the 23' class both in gaff and Bermudian rig, four of the 24' LOA, three of 25'LOA, two of 26' LOA, three of 28' LOA and one or two 31' LOA.

Reg Patten died in 1976 and his son Keith took over and continued to build dinghies, retiring in 2005 to pursue his hobby of restoring classic commercial vehicles.

The photos show various sizes of yachts built by Sea-King.

Above: Sea-King 23, Sea-King 26" • Below: Sea-King 24

Above: Sea-King 25'6" • Below: Sea-King 31

JOHNSON, SONS & JAGO
This company was building boats before the war, then known as Johnson & Jago until 1952/3 when they changed to Johnson Sons & Jago.

In the 1930s they built a several yachts, in 1938 'Tai Feng' a 31'Bermudian Cutter and 'Wings' an 18 footer both designed by R F Freeman. In 1938 they also built 'Suka' a 28.4' Bermudian Cutter designed by Maurice Griffiths and they built a number of Maurice Griffiths designs after the war.

During the war years they built some large wooden power craft such as 'Diahla' 112' in 1942 and 'Abingdon' 121' in 1945.

MIKE DAVIES

JOHNSON, SONS & JAGO LTD.
Leigh Marshes Leigh-on-Sea Essex Tel : 0702 76639

In the 1950s with the pleasure market developing again after the war, they built a number of their own 2.5 ton auxiliary sloops as shown in the drawings.

BERMUDIAN 2¼ ton AUXILIARY SLOOP

Builders JOHNSON SONS & JAGO LIMITED
SHIP & YACHT BUILDERS

THE BOATYARDS, LEIGH-ON-SEA, ESSEX
TELEPHONE : 76639 LEIGH-ON-SEA

Transport arranged
Price   Ex works
Insurance rates quoted on request

SPECIFICATION

Beam 7' 0"   •   Draft 3' 0"
L.O.A. 18' 0"   •   L.W.L. 17' 0"
Two Berth   •   Headroom 4' 9"

KEEL—English Oak, cut to shape and through bolted to iron keel.
STEM—English Oak. 3" Sided Moulded as plan.
STERN POST—English Oak, 3" Sided Moulded as plan.
TIMBERS—English Oak, 6" Centres steamed to shape.
PLANKING—Mahogany. ½" Copper fastened and rivetted.
SHELFING—Mahogany or Pine.
CARLINES—Oak or Pine.
DECK BEAMS—Oak or Pine.
FLOOR TIMBERS—English Oak, fastened through keel.
DECKING AND CABIN TOP—⅝" T & G matching canvas covered.
CABIN SIDES—Mahogany.
RUDDER—English Elm or Mahogany. Galvanised rudder gudgeons.
TILLER—English Oak.
COCKPIT SEAT—Mahogany or Pine
MOULDINGS AND TRIMMINGS—Mahogany.
SAILS — Bermudian rig.   Mainsail and Foresail (Jib extra).
MAST—Box Mast. Boom and Bowsprite.
PAINTING—Interior and Exterior, 3 coats of standard colour varnish, with white topside and black below floorboards and LWL.
EQUIPMENT—1 Galvanised Bow Anchor. 15 Fathoms of 1" Galvanised chain.
NAME—As required free of charge.

They also built a design by W Edward Wigfull – the 22' LOA Lynette Sloop, designed before the war.

They also built more of Maurice Griffith' designs, one of them the 5.5 ton auxiliary sloop.

In the 1970s in conjunction with Shuttlewoods at Paglesham they built a number of the Neptune and Neptunian glass fibre yachts designed by Alan Buchanan. They also built a Neptune 41 based on the Van de Stadt Victory 40 hull.

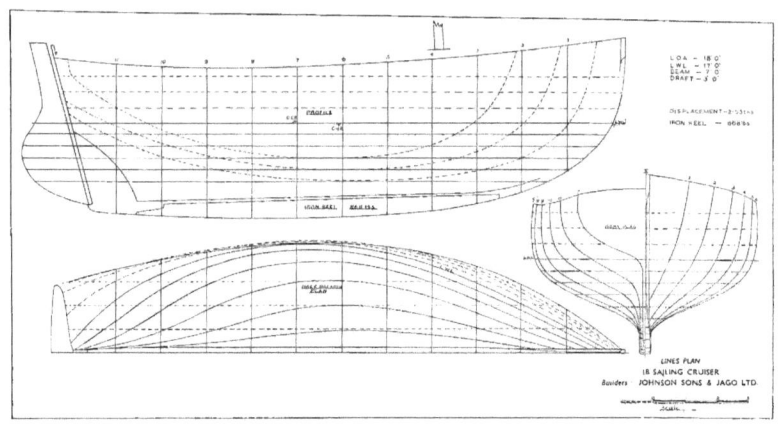

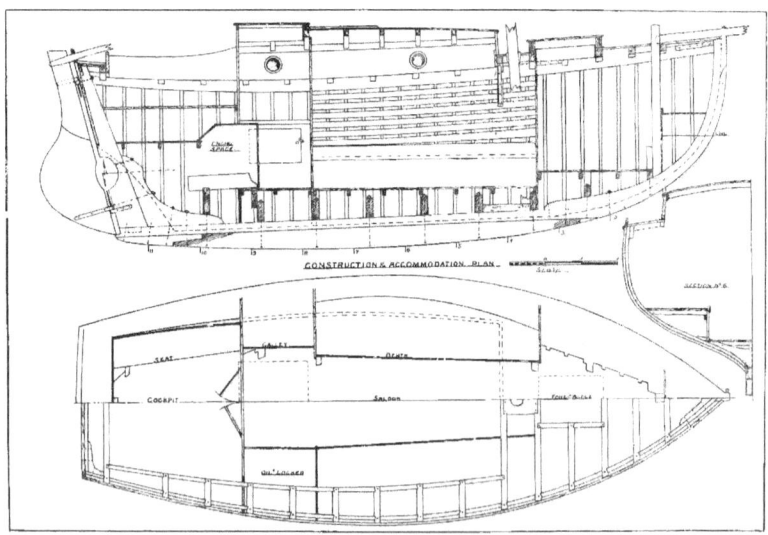

Johnson & Jago 2.5 ton sloop

Canvey Island

The Dauntless Company was originally located in Leigh-on-Sea in 1920, building dinghies and boats up to 30'. The yard was owned by 'Skip-

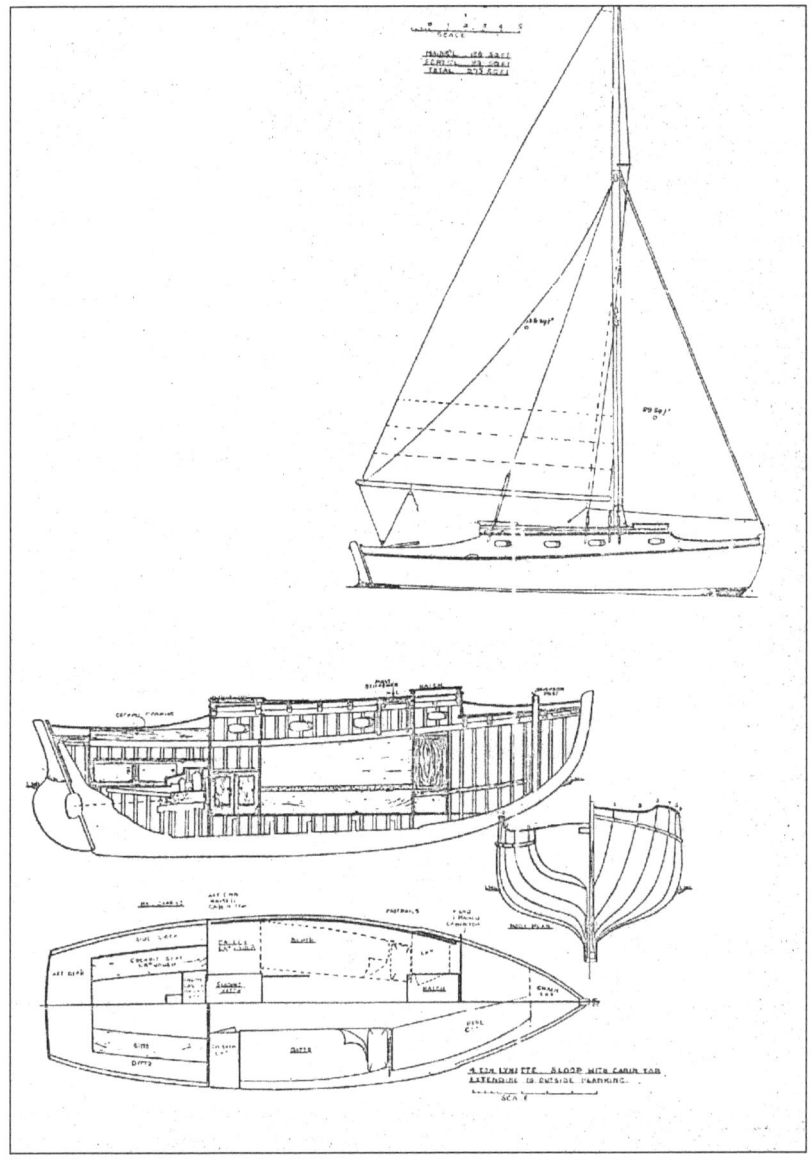

Lynette Sloop

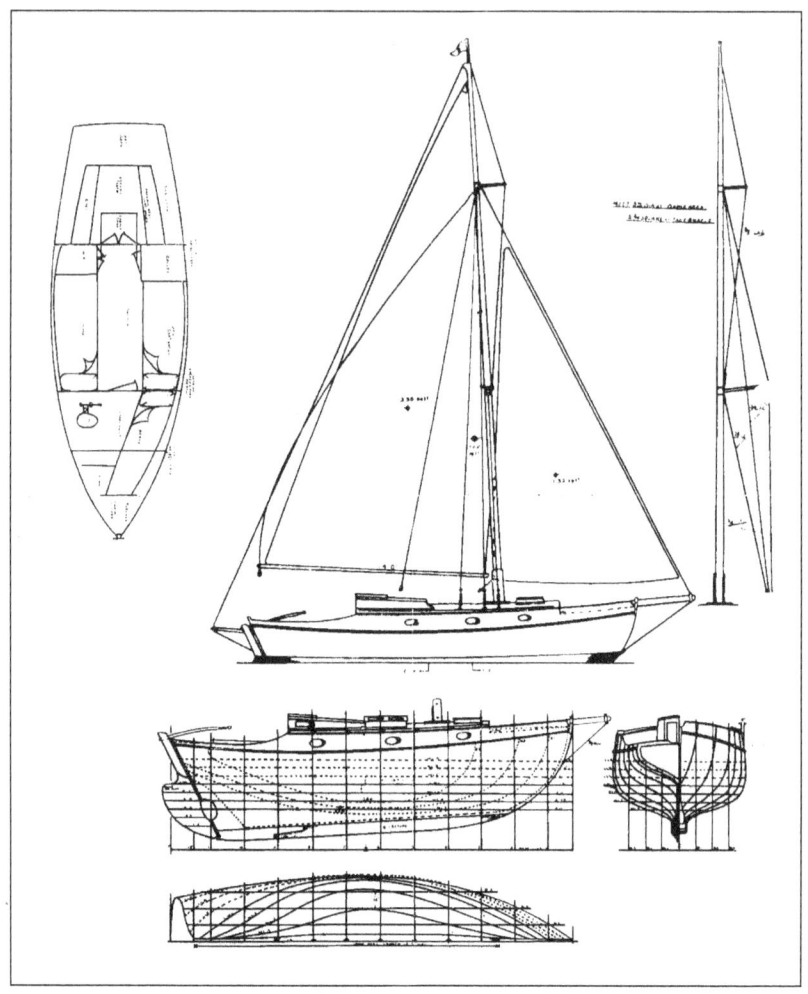

5.5 ton Sloop (possibly known as 'The Cockler')

per' Clayton and Reg Patten joined the company before the war as an apprentice.

At the outbreak of WWII the yard was moved to Severn Road Works, Welshpool, Montgomeryshire and built a number of whalers for the Admiralty.

At the end of the war, Dauntless moved back to Canvey Island and around 1946 starting building the Dauntless sailing yachts we know today. They were built two at a time and some of the staff at the time were Reg Patten (foreman), Sid Latimer (manager), Jonny Jones, Reg Wright and others.

They also built a 24' carvel fishing boat to a design by A G H Delgarno. Reg Patten left in 1958 to start his own business – Sea-King.

Fred Harris took over as foreman and the shape of the Dauntless changed with a more raked bow and more planks each side to give greater headroom.

The company was taken over by Sid Latimer (originally manager) and later his son Peter came into the business.

Dauntless also built motor cruisers – two are shown below.

Around 1979 Dauntless built an 18'GRP motor launch with small cuddy forward.

Dauntless 22 Gunter Rig

ESSEX AND SUFFOLK BOATYARDS AND BOAT BUILDERS

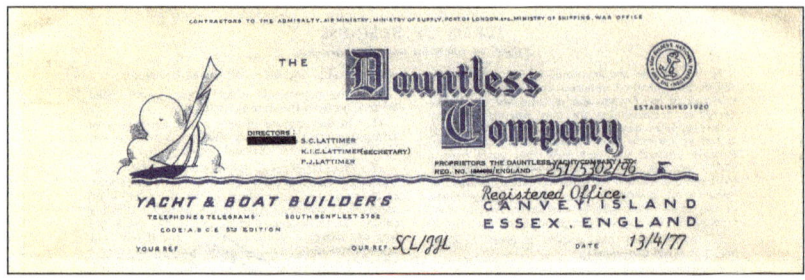

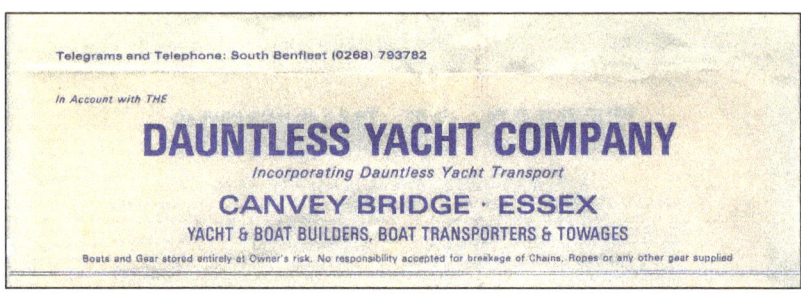

Dauntless 23 Gunter Rig

Typical Dauntless sailing yacht

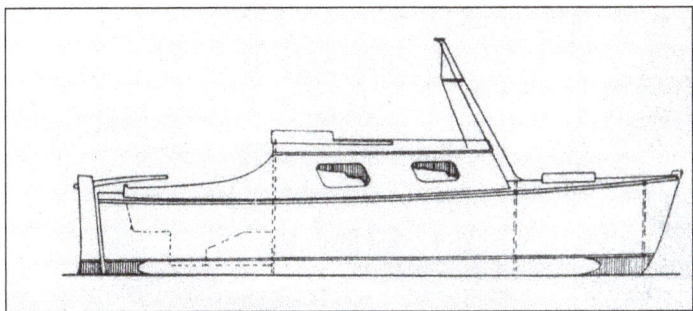

Dauntless 18 Motor Cruiser

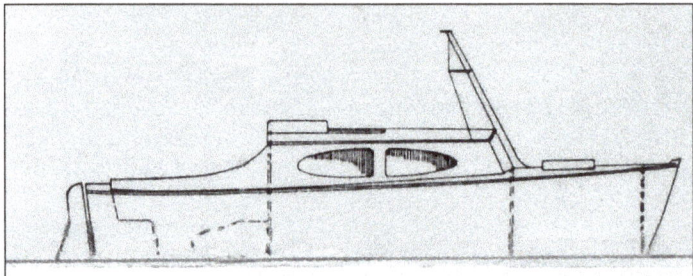

Dauntless 21 Motor Cruiser

Dauntless 18' Grp Launch

Alacrity, Vivacity and Jaguar Yachts

With the advent of glass reinforced plastic came boat builders who produced prolific numbers of yachts.

One of these was Eric Birch who owned Alacrity Yachts in the early 1960s and Russell Marine and Canvey Yacht Builders.

The Alacrity 19 was designed by Peter Stephenson in 1960 and trials of the first boat took place in late 1961.

It was originally built by Hurley Marine and marketed as a Hurley. From 1972 Russell Marine built all their own yachts.

The Mk II followed shortly after with two windows in each side of the coachroof.

The Alacrity was stretched by 18" to become the Vivacity 20/610, designed by D C Pollard and there were the Vivacity 21/670 and Vivacity 24/720 (designed by Alan Hill).

Russell Marine joined forces with Catalina Yachts in the USA - the Alacrity 22/670 (1970) was later known as the Jaguar 22 in UK and Catalina 22 in the USA and Lynx in France.

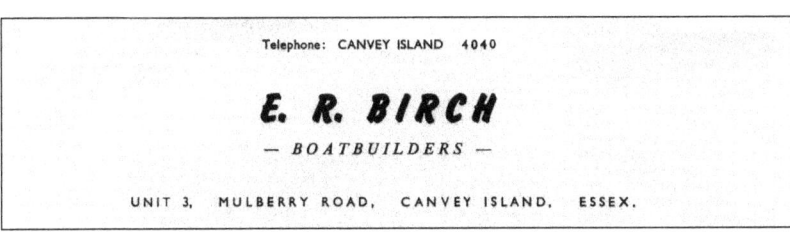

Alacrity Weekender　　　　　　Alacrity Mk II

Russell Marine eventually renamed themselves as Jaguar Yachts and produced the following range. (including but not shown Jaguar 22(Alacrity 22), Jaguar 265).

Jaguar 21

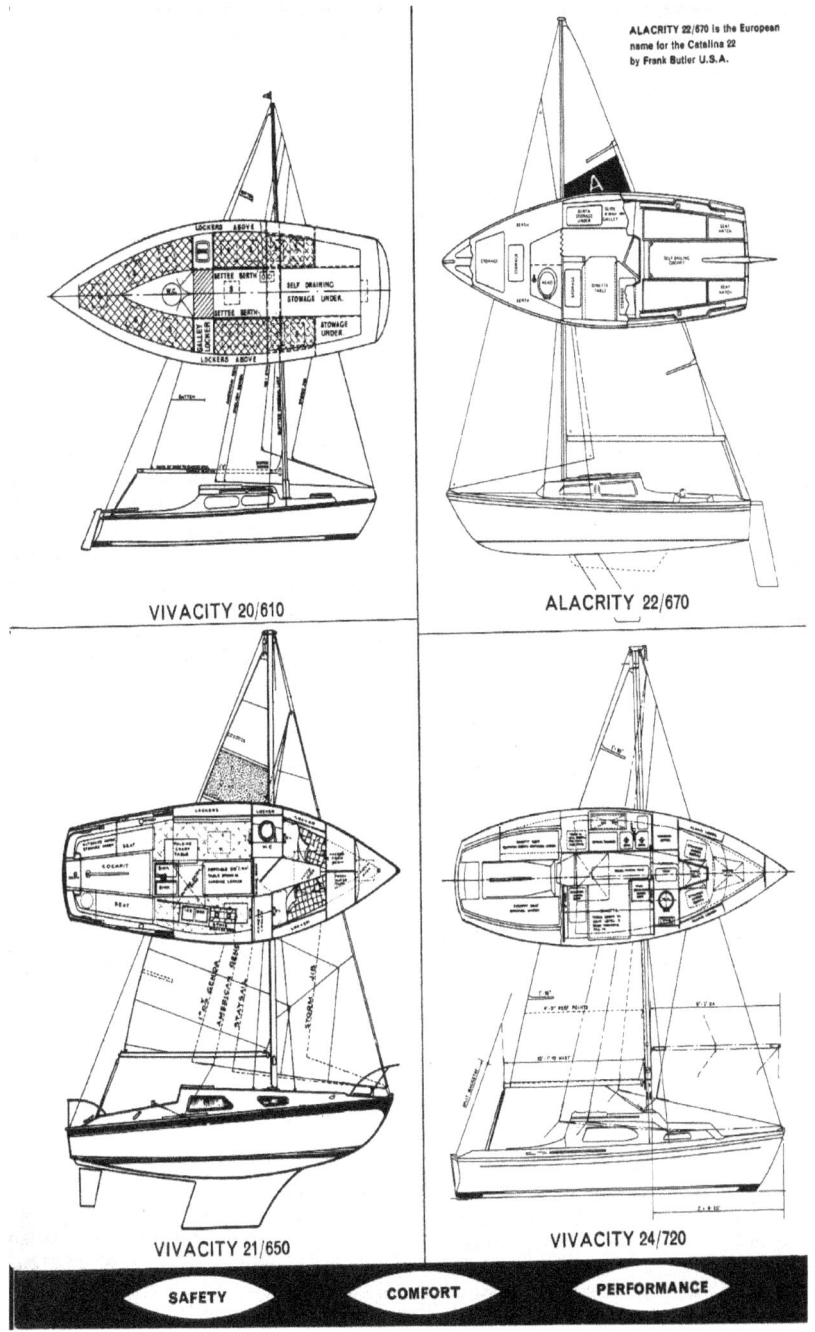

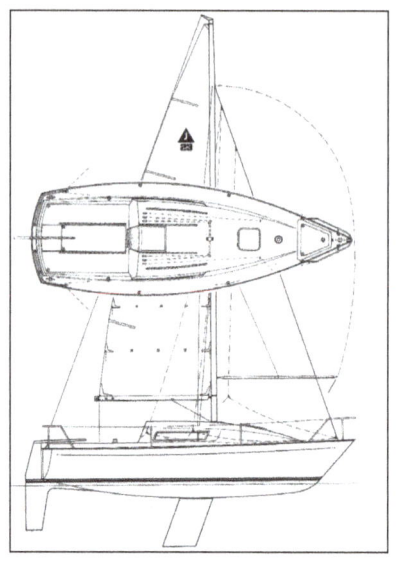 

Jaguar 23 C/R   Jaguar 25 (and Mk II)

Jaguar 27 (and Mk II)

Jaguar 30

After many years in production and hundreds of yachts produced the company finally ceased trading and Eric Birch worked as a consultant to Prout Catamarans, also on Canvey Island.

THAMES STRUCTURAL PLASTICS LTD

Thames Structural Plastics Ltd was formed in 1959 by Len Wakefield and Ray Walsh, starting business on a disused army site in Rayleigh. They set out to build boats, and other glass fibre products such as vehicle mouldings and furniture. It was the boats, which proved the most successful. The first three years produced small sales figures but expansion gradually took place and in 1962 they moved to Southend-on-Sea to larger premises.

This is a later letterhead around 1965.

The first yacht they produced was the Snapdragon 23 in 1962, a centreboarder which was popular with local sailing clubs.

In 1964 larger premises were needed and they moved to Canvey

Island. This was expanded in three stages from 1965, 1966 and 1967 to around 52,000 sq ft.

Snapdragon 23

It was at this time that they decided to simplify their trading name to TSP Marine Ltd and the name Thames Marine was used for marketing (see later Thames Marine (Mirage Yachts).

The company began taking on mouldings for other yachts, such as Halcyon 27 and Friendship whilst continuing their own lines.

In 1968 a GP 14 Dinghy License was granted and proved to be a popular line – with over 8,000 of the class in the world, not surprising.

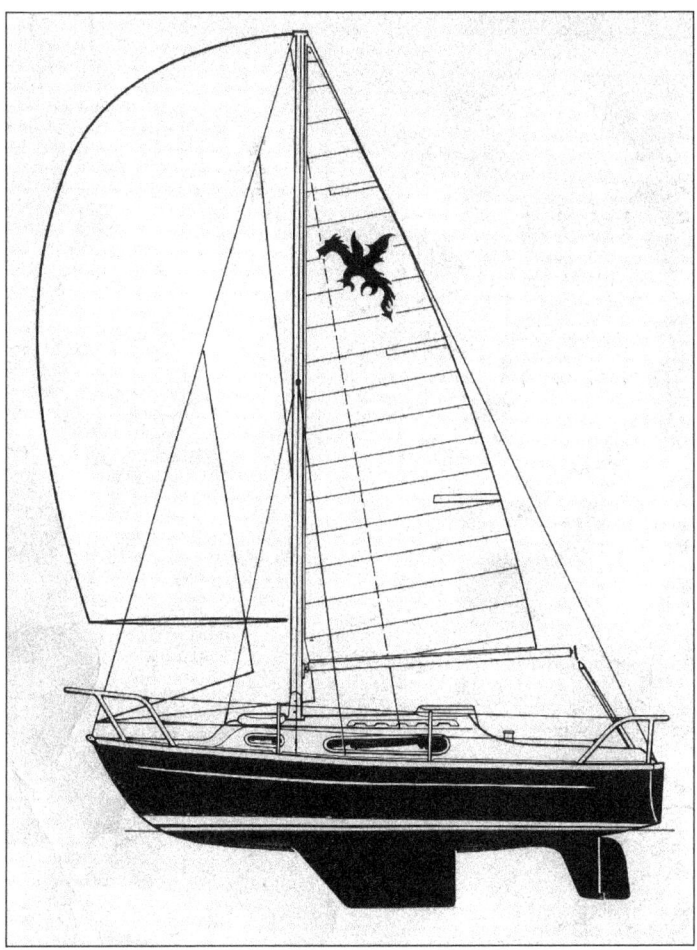

Snapdragon 21

At the 1970 Boat Show Thames Marine produced their own dinghy, the 11' Turtle, available in both kit form and complete versions. Some 350 were produced in the first year.

In the autumn of 1970 a sister company to Thames Marine was formed called Power Marine, to market the motor boats produced by TSP Marine. The Pacific 550 cabin cruiser was the first and sold well at home and abroad. This was followed by the Pacific 550 Dory and a 21' 4 berth cruiser, the Pacific 625 – plans were in hand for a 31' cabin cruiser.

At about the same time another company was formed with the Prout Brothers, Prout Marine, to market catamarans (See Prout Catamarans later).

Snapdragon 26   Snapdragon 747

Under the Thames Marine banner the Snapdragon 21 was produced. Also the Snapdragon 26.

In the 1970s production models included the Snapdragon 600, the Snapdragon 670, the Snapdragon 24 and it's updated version the Snapdragon 747.

Snapdragon 27   Snapdragon 890

Two larger yachts also formed part of the Snapdragon fleet – the Snapdragon 27 and the Snapdragon 890

Thames Marina (Mirage Yachts) and Boating Scene

Around 1975 Thames Marine started building the Mirage range of glass fibre yachts, mainly designed by David Feltham and originally based at Charfleet, Canvey Island, but moving later to High Road Laindon, Basildon.

The first yacht to be built was the successful Mirage 28, a cruising yacht available in bilge keels or fin keel configurations. Yachting Monthly wrote a report on this yacht in June 1976 by which time some 60 were on order with sixty percent destined abroad. By 1979 the Mirage 28 Mk II was in production.

All the Mirage range of yachts was to be available in kit form or fully completed craft. At around the same time the Mirage 37 was launched, a large cruising yacht with walk through to the aft double cabin with en suite heads. This was also available in twin bile keels or fin keel. A large volume yacht capable of sleeping seven with 6' 2" headroom.

In 1976 the Mirage 26 appeared, offering family cruising again with a choice of bilge keels or fin keel.

The Mirage 30 was being built by 1979, on similar lines and format to the 28 and 26 but available in bilge keel format only. This yacht had an aft cabin with two berths, a double dinette in the saloon and two V-berths in the fore cabin.

Two new models appeared, the Mirage 270 and Mirage 305.

The Mirage 270 was a new design will fuller hull, wider beam and again came in bilge keel or fin keel versions.

The Mirage 305 again was a new design and had a separate owner's double cabin aft, two settee berths in the saloon and two berths foreward.

Boating Scene bought the Leisure name and built the 27SL, derived from the Mirage 27 around 1989.

Thames Marine
Charfleet, Canvey Island, Essex. Telephone 03743 · 2228 Telex 995701 . ICC 136

BOATING SCENE
High Road, Laindon
BASILDON, Essex. SS15 6DS
Telephone: Basildon (0268) 540405

ESSEX AND SUFFOLK BOATYARDS AND BOAT BUILDERS

Mirage 28

Mirage 26

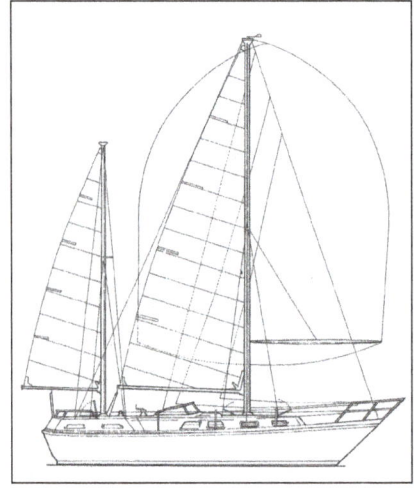
Mirage 37

Mirage 30

Prout Catamarans

Geoffrey Prout had established a boatbuilding business constructing folding dinghies and canoes and cold moulded dinghies in the late 1940s. This advertisement appeared in catalogue for the Second International Boat Show held at Olympia from December 1956 – January 1957.

The company was then named Geoffrey Prout and Sons and later changed to Prout Catamarans.

Mirage 305   Mirage 270

Geoffrey's two sons, Francis and Roland had been part of the K2 canoe team in the 1952 Olympics in Helsinki.

In 1947 two canoe hulls were joined together to form a catamaran and after some development the Shearwater catamaran appeared in Mk I form in 1954 with a dagger board placed centrally in the bridge deck. The Mk II followed in 1955 and then the very successful Shearwater Mk III. I owned and sailed a Mk III at Grafham Water in the mid 1960s, by which time it had hinged alloy centreplates in each hull.

Francis and Roland Prout developed the company, producing a large range of catamarans.

In 1956 they built 'Snow Goose' which three times won the Round the Island race held annually at Cowes, Isle of Wight.

They built a 19' cruising catamaran in 1961 named the Prout 19 Cabin Catamaran.

Designed to sleep four it had a lift up

G. PROUT & SONS LTD.
THE POINT, CANVEY ISLAND, ESSEX, ENGLAND, Tel: Canvey Island 190

cabin top and had a performance equal to that of the Shearwater III. To prevent total inversion if capsized, a 'Henderson' float was attached to the masthead.

In 1962 'Morima II' was built – being 40' long and 18' in the beam.

Also in 1962 they built the popular Prout 27 Ranger in glass fibre.

In 1964 the Prout 37 was built, the hulls moulded in six layers of mahogany and the rest in plywood.

On 14th July 1965 the largest catamaran to be built in Europe was launched, measuring 77' LOA with a beam of 24' and draft of 2' 10" and 6' 6" with plates down. The hulls were constructed in 5 laminations of wood, the inner one being 0.25" teak vertically laid, then 0.25" diagonal teak, 0.5" cedar laid fore & aft and 0.25" teak again vertically laid and finally a skin of 0.25" mahogany laid diagonally, all of which were covered in glass fibre up to 2' above the waterline.

1967 saw the Ocean Ranger built – 45' LOA with a beam of 20', all built in glass fibre.

Designs changed in these later catamarans with the mast being placed amidships giving a large fore triangle and small mainsail. A central nacelle (or canoe type body) was built in under the bridge deck which reduced hull slamming in heavy weather and provided good space for an inboard engine.

Around 1974 the Snow Goose 34 appeared with these features.

The Snow Goose 37 appeared around 1979, again with the now accepted Prout rig and hull shapes.

The Quest 31 was produced at this time.

The Sirocco 26 was also being built as a replacement for the earlier Prout Ranger 27 production of which had ceased eight years earlier.

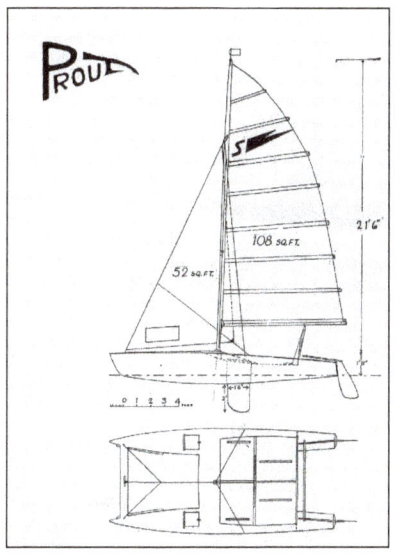
Shearwater Mk III

Snow Goose

Prout produced a large number of catamarans including one which was unique in having a mast stepped on each hull. Also they produced the Quasar, a 49' catamaran with a 20'beam and 1000sq ft of sail – a powerful boat.

In the 1980s they built the Scamper, a 26'cat with accommodation in

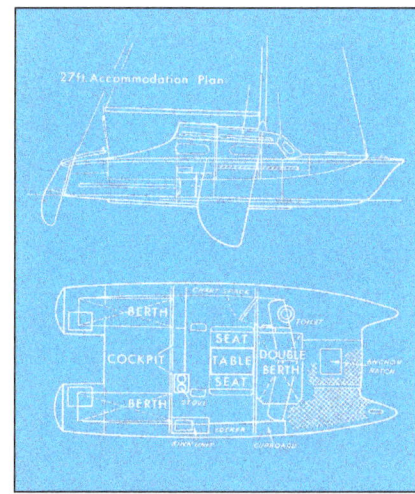

Prout 27 Ranger

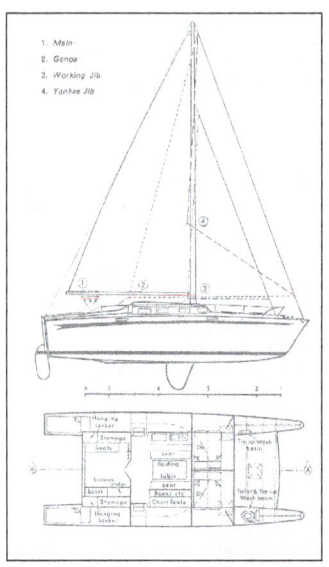

each hull and an open bridge deck.

Later they produced the Prout 45 in 1996. A fully fitted cruising catamaran which displaced 10 tonnes.

The business has now ceased trading after many years of business.

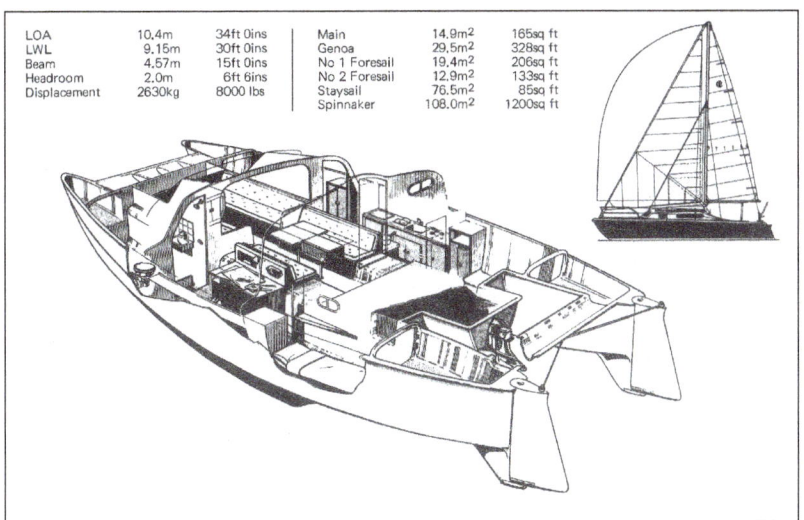

Prout Snow Goose 34

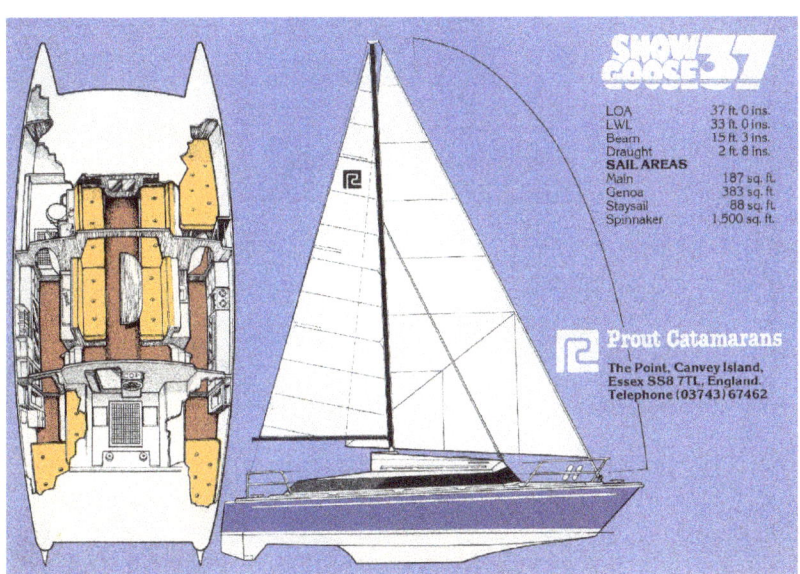

Prout Snow Goose 37

Prout Quest 31

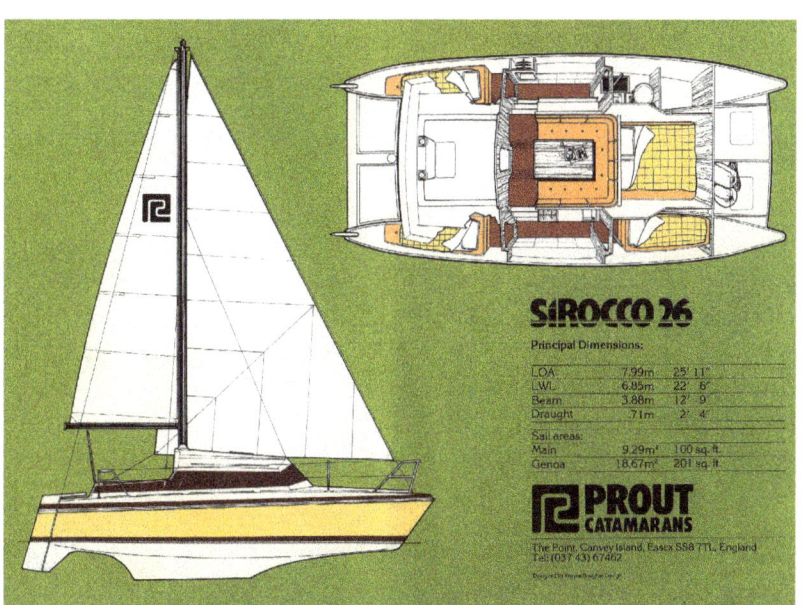

Prout Sirocco 26

CHAPTER 10
REFLECTIONS

AS CAN BE SEEN FROM the forgoing chapters, the East Coast has for many years been an area where ships and commercial craft have been constructed and later a great variety of pleasure craft built.

The influences of shape and design have come from the early settlers like the Vikings and Saxons and as people sailed the high seas to foreign ports, ideas were brought home to be incorporated into the designs of commercial and pleasure craft.

In the short time that the author has resided and worked on the East Coast, he has seen great changes in the use of commercial vessels on the rivers and creeks resulting in an almost total decline of working craft like the Thames Barge and fishing smack.

Many tidal rivers have also lost commercial trade but as this declined, people were gaining more leisure time and money to enjoy it.

Yachting used to be a rich man's sport as witnessed by the very large yachts built in the late 1800s and early 1900s.

Between the World Wars saw an increase in yacht building but it was after the Second World War that the largest changes took place.

Coming out of the austere years following the war, boat building started again. Many of the yards had of course been building vessels of all description for the Admiralty during the war.

Some of the expertise and materials developed during the war were used in boat building. Plywood and special glues appeared and many designs in plywood were built. Also, a surplus of naval craft were disposed of and were snapped up to be used as yachts – these included naval cutters, whalers and lifeboats. Remember that old converted lifeboat lying in a mudberth in some creek?

At the end of the 1950s a totally new material appeared – glass fibre. Once a mould was built many hulls and decks could be moulded quickly and with less labour. This new material opened the doors to cheaper yachts and the industry grew quickly with a new type of boat owner now being able to afford a yacht.

Ferro cement made a brief appearance in the 1960s and 1970s but declined as did steel and alloy although very large yachts in various parts of the world are now built in alloy. The Dutch have built yachts for many years in steel.

The current material for mass production, glass fibre and polyester resin is directly related to the oil industry and as oil becomes more and more expensive so the price of yachts will rise. What the future holds for the industry and boat buying public remains to be seen.

ACKNOWLEDGEMENTS

WITH THANKS TO ALL WHO offered help and information in compiling this book and especially these listed below, some of whom died before it was published.

Ian Brown	Peter Brown	Colin Burns
George Clark	George Collins	'Mouse' Green
Derek & John Halls	Guy Harding	Gayle Heard
Frank Hodgson	Alan Hill	Cyril Hughes
Mike Illingworth	Willem In't Veld	Frank Knights
James Lawrence	John Leather	Trevor Moore
Ernie Nunn	Vic Pascoe	Keith Patten
Peter Pearson	Alan Platt	Jim Spencer
John Swinton	Brian Upson	Russell Upson
Mary Waller	Andrew Wheatley	Peter Wilson
George Whisstock	Cyril White	Reg White
Stephen Whiteman	Ron Wyatt	

And my brothers Peter, Robin, Richard and Anthony.

INDEX

d = drawing   p = photo

Aldeburgh & Alde	30	Bradwell 18	136p, d
A F Platt Ltd	183, 185p	Bradwell 22 Fishing Cruiser	137p
Abingdon 121'	190	Bradwell 28	137d
Admiral Wyatt	111	Bradwell Marina	130p
Alacrity 19	199	Bradwell-on-Sea	131
Alacrity Mk II	200p	Brightlingsea	79p
Alacrity Weekender	200p	Brightlingsea LNER	
Alacrity Yachts	198	Passenger Ferry	104p
Alan III	56p	Brightlingsea One Design	80
Albatros Class (steel)	168	Brinecraft Ltd	90
Aldeburgh Boatyard	34p	British Folkboat	
Aldous & Son	79	Alan Hill design	152d
Aldous Shipyard	79	*British King Thames Barge*	143
Altair 1909	173	Brookes Claude	71
Anderson Mr	171	Brown Ian	107
Andy Harman	94	Brown Peter	73
Anglia Yacht Services Ltd	143	Brown Reg	38
Anstey Colin	113	Bryants Boats Bedford	22 p
Apache Cat	89p, 89d	Buchanan Alan	57, 107
Ardleigh Laminated Plastics	121	Budworth David	93
Arklight II	133	Bundock Thomas	188
Australis A Class Cat	87d, 87d	Burnham Yacht Building	
Barcarole Class Sula	188	Company	169
Barke David	160	Burnham Yacht Harbour	
Barker Charles (Dixon Kerly)	149	Marina Ltd	178d
Barnes Dennis	93	Burnham-on-Crouch	177
Bawley (ferrocement)	179d	Burns Colin (Colvic)	121
Beagle (Charles Darwin)	154	Butt & Oyster Pub, Pinmill	61p
Beckett Roger	143	*Buttercup Robert Clarke design*	104p
Bedwell & Co	75p	C H Fox & Sons	36
Bigmore Andrew	175	C H Fox & Sons Ltd, Ipswich	62
Birch Eric	199	Cannell David	109
Bird of Dawning	158	Canvey Yacht Builders	199
Blackwater 40		*Cap Pilar Barquentine*	97
(Colvic Mouldings)	147d	Cardenell G E	133
Blackwater 48 Trawler Yacht	141	Cardy Noddy	149
Blackwater Estuary	117	Cardnell Bros	133, 133p
Blackwater Marina	140, 141p	*Casquet*	107
Blackwater Sloop		Caterelle Ltd	149
(earlier & later versions)	153p	CB Boats	117
Blackwatwer 38 Trawler Yacht	134p	*Celandine 37' Gaff Ketch*	107
Blackwatwer 44 Trawler yacht	134p	Centre Board Ketch 40'	
Blue Bonnet	176	(ferrocement)	180d
Boating Scene	207	Chandler & Smith	161

Cherokee Cat	89p, 89d
Chittabob ECOD	172
Clark George (lock keeper)	139
Clark Pain J	172
Clark Robert	63, 107,173
Clarke & Carter Ltd	111, 114p
Clayton Skipper	194
Cleopatra 700 Sports Fisherman	*159p*
Cleopatra 850 Family Cruiser	*160p*
Cleopatra Range	*159*
Cobramould (Leisure Yachts)	89
Cockler 5.5 Ton Sloop	*194d*
Colchester	108
Cole Bill	171
Cole Bob	176
Cole Daniel	105, 111
Cole Joe	183
Cole Joseph	98
Cole Sonny	176
Cole Susannah	105
Colin Archer 40	*83d*
Colne Gaffer	*99*
Colne Marine & Yacht Company Ltd	100p
Colne Marine New Homes	101p
Colvic 19' 6" launch	*121p*
Colvic 20 Sailer	*121*
Colvic 23 m/s	*121*
Colvic 26' 6" m/c	*126d*
Colvic 29'6" Sailer	*121*
Colvic 31 m/s	*122d*
Colvic 34'6" Watson	*123p*
Colvic 38 Trawler Yacht	*124d*
Colvic 44 Sunquest	*126p*
Colvic Bluewater 476	*125p*
Colvic Countess 28	*123d*
Colvic Countess 37	*123d*
Colvic Craft Ltd	121
Colvic Range	*121*
Colvic Sailer 26	*122d*
Colvic Salty Dog 27	*121*
Colvic Salty Pup 23	*121d*
Colvic Seaworker 22	*126d*
Colvic Springtide 24	*121*
Colvic UFO 27	*124d*
Colvic Victor 34	*124d*
Comanche Cat	*88*
Cook & Woodward	143
Cook Samuel	103
Cook Walter	142
Corista	*43p*
Cornish Crabbers	167
Cornish Diva	167
Cox & King	99
Cox 12m	*82*
Cox 21	*82*
Cox 22	*84d*
Cox 27	*82*
Cox Brothers, Ipswich	82
Cox Marine Ltd	83p
Cox Master Mariner	*84d*
Crab & Winkle Railway	116
Cray Fishing Boat, Western Australia	*25p*
Crouch Engineering	175
Curgel A R G	39
Curtis Gus	59
Curtsey	*107*
Cutts Harold	113
Cutts Polly	113
Cyril White	81p
Dabchicks Sailing Club	112
Dallimore Norman	172, 176
Dan Wedd & Feesey Ltd	143, 144p
Darby Peter A	39
Darwin Charles	154
Dauntless 18' GRP Launch	*198p*
Dauntless 18 Motor Cruiser (wood)	*197d*
Dauntless 21 Motor Cruiser (wood)	*198dp*
Dauntless 22 Gunter Rig	*195d, 197p*
Dauntless 23 Gunter Rig	*196d*
Dauntless Company	196p
Dauntless Motor Cruiser (wood)	*198p*
David Budworth Ltd, Harwich	51
David Thomas	167
Davies Michael, Robin, Anthony Boat Show 1969	24p
Davies Mike canoe race	138p
Davies Norman & Mary	13
Dawn Thames Barge	*143*
Debbage Dennis	64
Debbages Yacht Services, Ipswich	64p, 65p
Deben 4 Tonner	*43d*

ESSEX AND SUFFOLK BOATYARDS AND BOAT BUILDERS

Deben 6 Tonner	*43d*	Ferguson Paul	136
Deben Cherub	*40p*	Ferro Cement Marine Services	179
Delphine ECOD	*172*	*Finesse 21*	*184, 186p,*
Diahla 112'	*190*	*Finesse 24*	*184, 186p*
Dione	*158*	*Finesse 27 (28)*	*185, 186p*
Dixon Kerly	148, 151p	Flack, John	95
Dodo 33.2' twin scew lug rig	*143*	*Flying Fifty 1953*	*63*
Donohoe Ray	107	Ford Marine (Clacton) Ltd	76
Donyland Shipyards Ltd	105	Forrest & Sons Ltd	96
Dragon Class (GRP)	*172*	Foster, Lewis Penrose	105
Dragon Class (wood)	*172*	*Fox 35 Ketch*	*63d*
Drake Alfred	116	Fox Uffa	63
Drake Brothers Tollesbury	116	Fox's Marina, Ipswich	62, 62p
Duck Punt	*117p*	Francis Jones J	42, 93
Duellist 32	*77dp*	Frank Halls & Son	71, 72p
Dyke Jonathon	58	Frank Knights	
East Anglian	*93*	(Shipwrights) Ltd	41p, 42p
East Anglian Restricted Class	*150d*	Fred Webb Ltd, Pinmill	60p
East Coast One Design	*172*	Freeman R F	190
East Mersea	13	French John	181
Edmond Colin (lock keeper)	139	Frost & Drake	118p
Elgris 1933	*62*	Frost Tom	117
Eliane 59	*59*	Furness Ivan	161
Elusive Lady	*176*	G Rennie & Co	97
Emmett Michael (Ostrea Rose)	140	G.F.Smeeth, Dedham	56p
Eridani II	*113*	Game Moses	95
Essex Boat Company (Hunter)	163	Garget Ken	181
Essex Boatyards	160	*Gelasma BOD*	*80p*
Essex Boatyards Ltd	161	Geoffrey Prout & Sons	208
Essex Marina	161, 161p	Gibson Power Craft	99
Essex Waterways Ltd	139	Giles Laurent	58
Essex Yacht Builders Ltd	159	Gliksten J & Co	97
Ethel Ada (Thames barge)	*155*	Goldie John	118
Everson & Sons Ltd	39p	Goldie Julian	119
Everson A M	39	Goodwin Malcolm	80, 99
F J Prior	173	*Gossip 41' gaff cutter*	*105*
F W Shutlewood & Sons	156	Gowen A A	113
Fairmile B Class	*133*	Gowen Ken	113
Fairmile D Class	*133*	Gowens Sailmakers	113, 113p
Falcon 17	*121*	*GP14 sailing Dinghy*	*204*
Fambridge Yacht Haven	182p	Green Trevor (Mouse)	118
Fanfare	*115*	*Grenade L Giles design*	*133*
Febris Marine	187	*Grethe GRP BOD*	*80p*
Felixstowe Docks	49p	Griffin Barry	114
Felixstowe Ferry Boatyard	36p, 36	Griffin Nick	114
Fellowship Afloat	118	Griffiths Maurice	40, 58
Feltham David	207	*Guy Thompson Quarter Tonner*	*63d*
Ferguson Brothers (Bradwell) Ltd	136	Halls Alf	71

Halls Christopher	75	Horlocks Mistley	54p
Halls Derek	73	Horlocks Mistley	54
Halls Frank	71	Houston Family	105
Halls John	73	Howard Arthur	89
Halls Trevor	75	Howard John	143
Harbottel Laurie	184	Hudson Bay Company	95
Harbour Marine Services	31p	*Hunter 19*	*163*
Harding Guy	99	*Hunter 21, 23, 30*	*166*
Hare Paddy	113	*Hunter 27, 272, 273*	*166*
Harman Andy	94	*Hunter Horizon 32*	
Harman Dick	94	*Wheelhouse Cruiser*	*166, 166p*
Harris Fred	195	*Hunter 490*	*163*
Harris James	103	*Hunter 701*	*169*
Harris Mr	103	*Hunter 707*	*169*
Harris Peter	103	Hunter Boats	169
Harrison Butler T	62	*Hunter Channel 31*	*169*
Harry King & Sons, Pinmill	58	*Hunter Channel 32*	*166*
Harvey Thomas	95	*Hunter Delta 25*	*165, 165p*
Harwich Harbour	48	*Hunter Europa II*	*164d*
Harwich Shipyard	48	*Hunter Horizon 26*	*165p*
Hawkins Williams	95	*Hunter Impala 28 OOD*	*165p*
Heard Gayle Sailmaker	119	*Hunter Jet Cruiser 20 (early)*	*167*
Hedgecock & Son	148	*Hunter Liberty 22*	*165*
Hedgecock Roger	148	*Hunter Medina 20*	*165*
Hedgecock Tom	148	*Hunter Minstrel*	*165p*
Heerde John de	116	*Hunter Pilot 27*	*167*
Hellcat Mk II	*85d*	*Hunter Ranger 245*	*167*
Hemmingway Mike	177	*Hunter Ranger 265*	*167p*
Hempstead Boatyard	114	*Hunter Sonata*	*164p*
Heron sailing dinghy	*184*	*Hunter Tracer*	*163*
Heybridge Basin	138p	Husk James	98
Hill Alan	76	Husk's Boatyard	98p
Hill Peter	181	Ian Brown Ltd	107
Hobie Cat 14	*24p*	*Ilala 1962*	*64*
Hodsdon John	181	Illingworth Mike	45
Holland Ron	64	Ingham Roy	39
Holliwell 21.5' Sloop	*141p*	In't Veld Willem	82
Holman & Pye	115	Ipswich Haven Marina	67
Holman & Pye	177	Ipswich Wet Dock	65p, 66p
Holman C R	107	*Iroquois II Cat*	*88d, 88p*
Holman Kim	115	*Iroquois Mk I Cat*	*87*
Holt & James	140	*Iroquois Mk IIa Cat*	*87*
Holt Arthur	140	J & H Cann, Harwich	52
Horlock Chubb	54	J King	169
Horlock F W	55	J W Shuttlewood & Sons	156
Horlock John	55	Jack Ward & Sons, Pinmill	60p
Horlock Peter	55	*Jacqueline Bawley*	*118*
Horlock, Richard	55	*Jaguar 21 (later)*	*200p*

ESSEX AND SUFFOLK BOATYARDS AND BOAT BUILDERS

Jaguar 22	199	Lawling Creek	133
Jaguar 23 C/R	202d	Lawrence Jimmy	82
Jaguar 25	202p	Laws G U	172
Jaguar 265	200	Leather John	57, 102
Jaguar 27	202p	Lee Oliver	163
Jaguar 30	203p	Leigh-on-Sea	188
Jaguar Yachts Ltd	199	Leisure 17	90p, 90d
James & Stone	80	Leisure 17SL	92p
James Cook & Co	98	Leisure 20	91p
Jennie	158	Leisure 22	91d
Jewel	80	Leisure 23	90
Jim Spencer Sailing Services	82	Leisure 23SL	92p
John Millgate	116p	Leisure 26 Elite	92p
Johnson & Jago		Leisure 27	91p
2.5 Ton Sloop	191d, 192d	Leisure 27SL	208
Johnson, Sons & Jago	191	Leisure 29	91
Jones F Morgan	116	Levanter	158
Jones Jonny	195	Lisbet	172
Jones Thornton	181	Listang	132d
Jubilee Trust STA	99	Lona III	172
Juxtamare Marine	131	London Boat Show Stand 1969	24p
K H Marine	84	London International Boat Show	24
Karen 1931	62	Lora 43' Schooner	20p, 21p
Kate (oyster smack)	155	Lord Nelson STA Ship	99
Keeble James	143	Lord Roberts Thames Barge	143
Kemp William	155	Lynette 22	193d
Kerly Dixon	149	Lyon-Hall J	171
Kestrel 22	72p, 73d	Lysander 17 (grp)	187d
Ketch 38' (ferrocement)	180d	Macalpine-Downie Rodney	87, 88
Kidby John	95	Macmillan James	140
King Morgan	172	Maid of Wyvern wood cutter	101p
King Stan	172	Malcolm Goodwin premises	98p
King William, Wivenhoe	95	Maldon Quay	142p
King William	172	MAM Ltd Bradwell Marina	131
Kirmew	172	Mapleleaf Sloop	162d, 162p
Knights Frank	41	Marine Traders Yacht	
Kulu	158	Brokers offices	27p, 28p, 29p
Kylix II M Griffiths	57p	Marlin	42
L H Walker	188	Marsh Rodney	85
La Cucararcha	158	Martlesham Creek Boatyard	38p
Lady Camelot	158	Maslen Frank Ernest	105
Landau 20	167	Matawa 37' 8" plywood yacht	
Landau 29 Continental	167	Morgan Giles	133
Landau Cruiser (Hunter)	167	Maverick (grp)	113
Landau Launch Company	167	Mayland Family Sixteen	135p
Larkman Dick	45	Mayland Fisherman Sixteen	135p
Latimer Sid	195	Mayland Marine	135
Laurent Giles & Partners	173	McMullen Major	117

Mel Skeet Granary		Nottage Maritime Institute	103p
Yacht Harabour	46, 47p	Nunn Ernie	37
Melton Boatyard Ltd	47p	*Nutshell dinghy*	99
Merganser	105p	*Nyala 1933 M Griffths*	40p
Merlander	113	*Oakleaf Sloop*	163p
Mersea One Design	19p	*Odd Times*	107
MFV	172	Oliver H Rice & Cole Ltd	171
Millgate John	115	Oliver Nick Rice & Cole Ltd	171
Mirage 26	208p	*Orange Pippin 1976*	64
Mirage 270	209d	Orford Quay	31p
Mirage 28	208p	Osea Island	135
Mirage 28 Mk II	207	*Ostrea Rose smack*	140p
Mirage 30	208p	Ouxley Family	105
Mirage 305	209d	Overbury Adrian	45
Mirage 37	208d	Oxton Walter	105
Mirage Yachts	207	*Oyster*	103
Mistley Marine	54p	Oyster Marine	109
Moiya sailing dinghy built		*Pacific 550 Cabin Cruiser*	205
Wm Wyatts	112p	*Pacific 625 cabin Cruiser*	205
Moliette (concrete 3 master wreck		Page Herbert	172
Cocum Hills)	179	Page Robert	95
Montague 27' Whaler	143	Paglesham Reach	155
Moore Trevor	36	Pascoe Vic (Colvic)	121
Morima II 40' Cat	210	Patten Keith	189
Mouse Green & premises	118p	Patten Reg	188, 189
MTBs	172	Pearce Barry	143
Mulberry harbour	97	Pearson Peter	181
Mystery 35	167	*Peregrine Sloop*	94p
National Squib	163, 164d	Peter B Clarke	114
Navaho 46' Cat	88d	*Peter Duck*	58, 59d
Naval House, Harwich	50p, 51p	Petrie Chris	75, 181
Nelson Horatio	49	Petticrows Ltd	171
Neptune Marina, Ipswich	66	Pettigrew Burnham-on-Crouch	81
Neptune Sloop	157d, 157p	*Phylla 23' 6" (larger version*	
Neptunian Ketch		*Blackwatwer Sloop)*	148p
Shuttlewoods	158d, 158p	Pinmill	58
Neptunian Ketch Johnson & Jago	191	*Piver Trimaran Cox Marine*	82
New Blossom class	103	Platt Alan	183
Newell Pettigrew	171p	Poland Peter	163
Nicholson C E	176	Port Flair Ltd	131
Nixon Peter & Chris	64	Port of Colchester	108
Nonsuch (1650)	95	Porter & Haylett	58
North Fambridge		Power Marine	205
Yacht Station	181, 182p	*Prior 30 Timba*	174p
North Sea 127	110p	Prior Frederick	173
North Sea Canners	101	Prior Murray	76, 173
North Sea Craft Ltd	108	*Prior Passge maker*	174p
Nottage Capt Charles G	102	Prior Reg	173

ESSEX AND SUFFOLK BOATYARDS AND BOAT BUILDERS

Prior Robin	174	River Stour	54	
Priors Boatyard	173	*RNLI Lifeboats*	107	
Property Associates	97	Robb Arthur	107	
Prout 19 Cabin Catamaran	210	Robertson A V	44	
Prout 27 Ranger	211dp	Robertson E J	44	
Prout 37	210, 212dp	Robertsons of Woodbridge Ltd	45p	
Prout Ocean Ranger 45 Cat	210	*Rodingen Folkboat 1941*	100p	
Prout 77' Cat	210	Root & Diaper	142	
Prout Catamarans	208	Rowhedge	103	
Prout Folding Dinghy	209p	Rowhedge Ironworks	105	
Prout Francis	209	*Royal Burnham One Design*	172	
Prout Geoffrey	209	Russell Marine Ltd	199	
Prout Marine	205	Rutter Mervyn	119	
Prout Quasar 49' Cat	211	*Sabrina fair*	176	
Prout Qust 31	214dp	Sail Lofts Tollesbury	120p	
Prout Roland	209	Sailcraft Ltd	85	
Prout Scamper 26 Cat	212	Sainty Philip	95	
Prout Sirocco 26	215dp	Sainty Philip	108	
Prout Snow Goose 34	212p, 213d	*Salar 40*	159	
Prout Snow Goose 37	213dp	Scattergood Colin	57	
Pryor Frank	90	*Scimitar (Whaler conversion)*	17d, 17p	
Puritan Smack	115p	*Scimitar (Whaler conversion)*		
Pye Donald	115	Heybridge Basin	18p	
Pyfleet Creek	78	Seacraft Leigh	184	
Queen Bee Masthead Sloop		SeaEnd Boathouse	171	
A K Balfour	151d	Seaking (Boatbuilders) Ltd	188	
Quiz, 1872 Smack	41p	*Sea-King 23*	189p	
R J Prior	173	*Sea-King 24*	189p	
R. Larkman Ltd	46p	*Sea-King 25' 6"*	189p	
Ramsholt Arms	37p	*Sea-King 31 Ketch*	190p	
Ramsholt Quay	37p	Seamaster	127	
Ranger 14 Dinghy	23p	*Seamaster Commander*	26, 27	
Ranger 14 Prototype			28, 127	
Sailing Dinghy	23p	*Seamaster 1123*	129	
Ranger 20 Rescue Launch		*Seamaster 19 yacht*	129	
(Colvic hull)	25P	*Seamaster 20 Captain*	127	
Ranger Boats	24	*Seamaster 21 power*	127	
Ransome Arthur	58, 68	*Seamaster 23 power*	127	
Ratcliffe Dr Walter	101	*Seamaster 23 yacht*	129d	
Red Fox Yachts	167	*Seamaster 24 Cadet power*	127	
Renown (fishing boat)	188	*Seamaster 25 Admiral power*	127	
Rice & Cole Ltd	170p	*Seamaster 29 yacht*	130p	
Rice Tom	170	*Seamaster 30 power*	129p	
Richardson C D (Dixon Kerly)	149	*Seamaster 34*	129	
Riggs Tom	57	*Seamaster 725*	127p	
River Crouch	167	*Seamaster 8 Metre power*	128p	
River Orwell	57	*Seamaster 813 power*	128p	
River Roach	154	*Seamaster 815 yacht*	129d	

Seamaster 820 power	*128p*	Stuttle William	108
Seamaster 925 yacht	*130d*	Suffolk Yacht Harbour Ltd	58p
Seamaster 950 power	*129*	*Suka Bm Cutter*	*190*
Seamaster Cub 17 power	*127*	*Sulaire 1933*	*62*
Secret	*158*	*Surian Too*	*161*
Select Yacht Group	167	Sutton & Smith	161
Seligman Adrian	97	Sutton & Wiggins Ltd	161
Sephine	*75*	Sutton E W	161
Shearwater Mk I & II Cats	209	Sutton Hoo	43
Shearwater Mk III Cat	210p, 211p	Suttons Boatyard	161
Shipways Yard Maldon	143	Swan Hunter &Wigham	
Shotley Marina Holdings Ltd	177	Richardson Ltd	105
Shotley Point Marina	53p, 54p	Swann Clint	140
Shuttlewood Frank	155	Swin Mouldings	136
Shuttlewood James	155	*Swin Ranger Ketch*	*84d*
Shuttlewoods Boatyard	155p, 156p	*Swin Ranger Mk 3*	*85p*
Skeet Mel	45	Swinton & Wilkinson	133
Skeet Simon	45	Swinton John	133, 144
Slaughden Quay	32 p	Swinton Richard	109
Smith Ken	177	*Tai-Feng 31'*	*190*
Snapdragon 21	*205d*	*Tamarisk 19*	*109p*
Snapdragon 23	*204p*	*Tamarisk 22*	*109p*
Snapdragon 24	*206*	*Tamarisk 24*	*109p*
Snapdragon 26	*206p*	Tartan Arrow Marine	159
Snapdragon 27	*206p*	*Thai Cat IV*	*86p*
Snapdragon 600	*206*	*Thames Estuary One Design*	*116*
Snapdragon 670	*206*	Thames Marine	204
Snapdragon 747	*206*	Thames Structural Plastics Ltd	203d
Snapdragon 890	*206*	The Chelmer Canal Trust	139
Snape Quay	34 p	The Old Chapel Wivenhoe	27p
Snow Goose Cat Prout	*211p*	The Old Naval Yard, Harwich	50p
Southwold Harbour	30	The Oyster Group	62
Spear Michael	58	The River Colne	78
Spitway	111	*The Whaler 25' Montague Davies*	
St Osyth Boatyard Ltd	93, 93p	*family*	*15d, 16d, 17d, 17p, 18p*
Standing Walter (Varne Marine)	152	*Thirza*	*161*
Stanley Austin	95	Thompson Guy	176
Stardrift	*107*	Thurtle Arthur	131
Starsong	*106*	Tide Mill Marina, Woodbridge	45p
Stebbens Boatyard	141p	Tide Mill, Woodbridge	44p
Stebbings	168, 168d	*Tideway 12*	*188*
Stella Class	*106d*	*Tideway 25 Peter Brown design*	*73p*
Stella Class	*176d*	*Timba Prior 30*	*75, 76p*
Stennet Charles	58	*Tiny Mite (small barge)*	*158*
Stickney Richard	181	Titchmarsh Marina Ltd	70p
Stone D & Sons	80	*Toad dinghy*	*99*
Storm Class	*184*	Tollesbury International Marine	119
Stuttle Westerby	108	Tollesbury Marina	119p

ESSEX AND SUFFOLK BOATYARDS AND BOAT BUILDERS

Tollesbury Yacht & Boat Building Company		116	Walton One Design	71
			Wanderer III (Eric Hiscock)	173
Tollesbury Yacht Berthing Company		116	Ward Tony & Christine	59
			Water Rat dinghy	99
Tollesbury		116	Waterhouse Jack	118
Tomahawk		100	Watts Capt O M	106
Tornado Cat		87d, 87p	Webb Dan	143
Treadmill Crane Harwich		49p	Wenonah	58
Trident Laminates Ltd		136	West Mersea	111
Trinity House		50	West Wick Marina	181
Trintella IIIA		74d	Weston 850	152
TSP Marine Ltd		204	Weston Boats	152
Tubbs W J (Dixon Kerly)		149	Whirlwind	115
Tucker Brown		170, 175, 175p	Whisstocks Ltd	42p
Tucker Jonathon		176	White Cyril	81
Tucker R J S (Stan)		175	White Formula Ltd	88
Tug Kelpie		51p	White Reg	85
Turtle 11		205	White Robert	88
Twister Class		115	White T C	80
Undine (probably first 18' Blackwater Sloop)		145d	Widgeon ECOD	172
			Wigfull W Edward	192
Upshall Richard		45	Wilkins E J	96
Upson Brian		33p	William Blake	42
Upson Russell		32,33	William King & Sons	172
Vanguard (oyster dredger)		173	William Wyatts Ltd	112p
Varne 27		153d	Wings 18	190
Varne 850		153d	Wiseman James	188
Varne Folkboats Ltd		152	Wivenhoe	94, 96p
Varne Marine		152	Wivenhoe Port Ltd	97
Vera Jane 1947		63	Woodrolfe Boatyard Ltd	119
Vertigan Malcolm		93	Woodward Arthur	143
Vertue Class L Giles design		133	Woolverstone Marina	61p
Victory 40		74	Worsp Louis	101
Vivacity 20/610		201d	Wright Eric	58
Vivacity 21/650		201d	Wright Reg	195
Vivacity 22/670		201d	Wyatt George	95
Vivacity 24/740		201d	Wyatt Ron	75
Vosper Ltd		97	Wyatt William	111
W M Blake		42	Yacht Haven Group	181
Wakefield Len		203	Yachting World Catamaran	86d, 86p
Waldringfield Boatyard Ltd		37p	Yardleys	169
Wallasea Island		159	Ylva 24 ton Yawl	100
Wallet		111	Yokesfleet Creek	155
Walsh Ray		203	Yuletide	173
Walter Cook & Son		142	Zorina (GRP)	177
Walton & Frinton Yacht Club Pool		70p		
Walton Backwaters Twizzle Creek		69p		